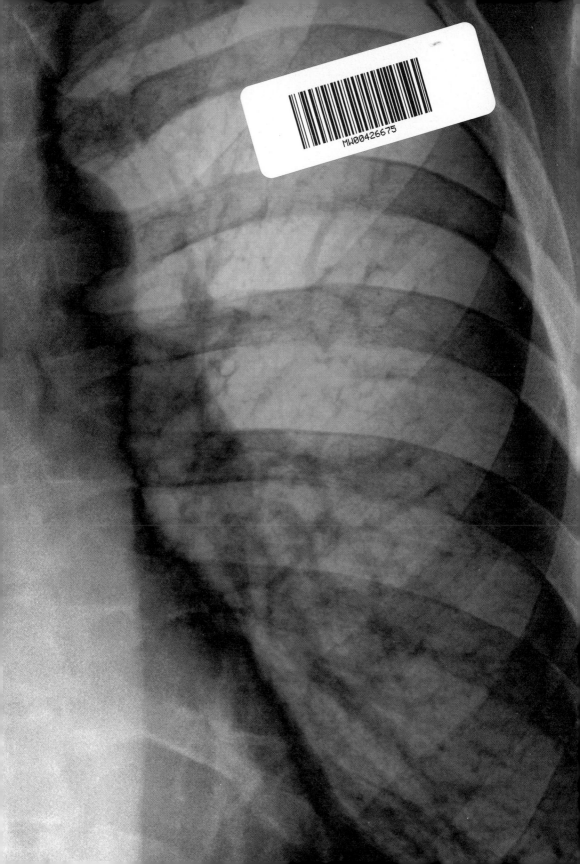

DESIGN THE INVENTION OF DESIRE

YALE UNIVERSITY PRESS | NEW HAVEN AND LONDON

AN OBSERVER EDITION

DESIGN THE INVENTION OF DESIRE

Jessica Helfand

Yale University Press books may be purchased in quantity
for educational, business, or promotional use. For
information, please e-mail *sales.press@yale.edu* (u.s.
office) or *sales@yaleup.co.uk* (u.k. office).

Designed by Jessica Helfand and Sara Jamshidi.

Set in Akzidenz Grotesk and Galaxie Copernicus.

Photography by George Baier iv.

Printed in China.

Library of Congress Control Number: 2015950947

isbn 978-0-300-20509-1 (cloth : alk. paper)

A catalogue record for this book is available from the
British Library.

This paper meets the requirements of ansi/niso
z39.48-1992 (Permanence of Paper).

10 9 8 7 6 5 4 3 2 1

This book is for Cornelia Holden and Kevin Hicks—for their humanity, their humility, and their boundless grace.

We all have the same inner life. The difference lies in the recognition.
Agnes Martin

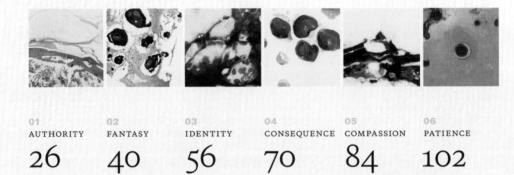

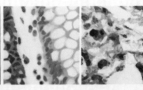

You can't invent a design. You recognize it, in the fourth dimension.
That is, with your blood and your bones, as well as with your eyes.

D. H. Lawrence

Introduction: Conscience

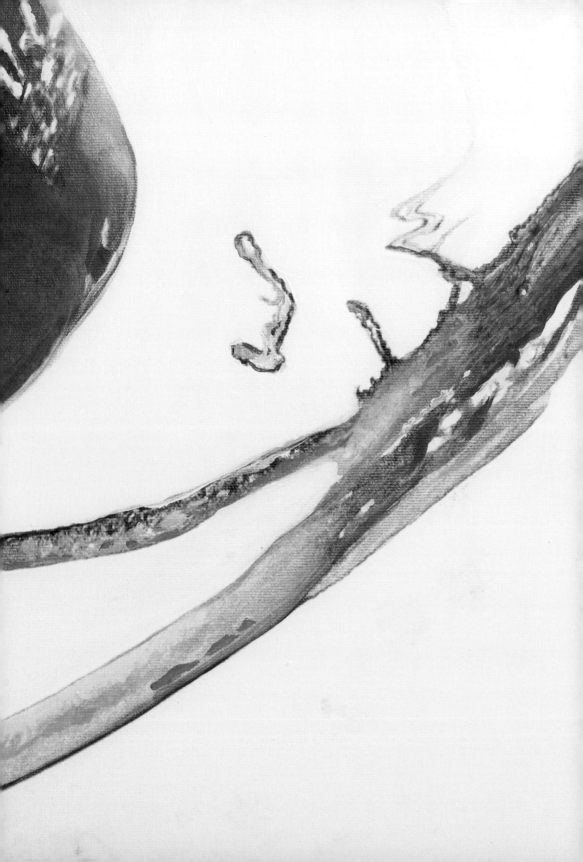

DESIGNERS ARE, BY THEIR VERY NATURE, EMISSARIES OF ALL THAT faces outward: makers, doers, propagators seeding the future. Their focus is on identifying and, by conjecture, improving the conditions that frame our experience, bringing order and efficiency, comfort and delight, entertainment, information, clarification to all that eludes us. More often than not, their purview is what's new, what's novel—what's *next*. The eyes are in constant operation, while the long-neglected soul is rarely, if ever, called into play.

If, for example, the eyes are the window to the soul—a statement that has been attributed to playwrights (like Shakespeare) and poets (like Milton), to the Bible (Matthew 6:22), and even to Cicero (he added the nose and the ears)—why do we favor the former at the considerable expense of the latter? The soul, of course, is an incomprehensible entity—planetary in its vastness and just as impossible to harness as, say, matters of taste or opinion. (These are perplexing concepts, at once distinctive yet intangible.) But let's return to the idea of what it means, for a sentient being, to respond to something for which the initial point of entry is a visual one. At a cellular level, physical responses are our most indelible human gestures. To look at something— a Rembrandt, a film, your child's beautiful face—is to have, first and foremost, a physical reaction. Your heart races. Your pulse quickens. Your central nervous system—that magnificent I beam connecting your heart to your brain—is cued into action, completing the trifecta that supports the human ecosystem, thus enabling you to look and feel. (And here you thought look and feel was a technological conceit.)

This is what it means to be alive—to witness visually and respond viscerally to something, and thus to act not because your parents said so, or your professor mandated it; not because it is popular or viral or trending; but because you engaged as an individual with a deeper understanding of what it means to contribute to a world not merely of your own making. Within the context of this essential gestalt, the eyes may be the first line of defense, but what you do afterward demands considerably greater scrutiny. What are the moral codes, the ethical parameters, the philosophical benchmarks that fuel our subsequent actions? And what of the wider ramifications that inevitably follow, when you make something and put it out into the world, influencing others, seeding the future?

The images in this book propose a parallel exploration, beginning with the biological truths to which we are, each of us, inevitably tethered. Each originates with a selected scientific image—a histology—which is to say, a biological sample of human tissue captured on a slide. These images are then projected or printed onto canvas and painted: protoplasms (an anatomical material) rendered through pigment (an aesthetic one). While they formally present as abstract images, they are, in fact, precisely the opposite, reminding us that at a molecular level, we all look pretty much the same. Heart muscle is heart muscle—at turns porous and sinewy, slick and thick. Dendritic cells are slender lines, like tree branches, that process antigens in the immune system. The image on the cover of this book is a teased nerve, and what is design if not just that—a live wire? ("Oh the nerves, the nerves," wrote Dickens in 1844. "The mysteries of this machine called Man!") These are visual metaphors, but they serve equally as compelling conceptual models. Just as the fibers of a nerve can regenerate, so too can we realign the coordinates that frame discussions of design in terms of what are, in fact, critical questions with vast and vital consequence. We can, and we must.

These paintings propose that at a certain fundamental level—somewhere between the reassurance of scientific certainty and the delight of formal abstraction—we are all united, and that it is within this stunning visual vocabulary of biological beauty that we present as a species. To participate in that understanding, and to observe the simultaneously specific and epic ramifications of what are, in the end, the microscopic cells that give us life, is a piercing reminder that we are all reducible to something extremely concrete, something deeply primal and inordinately gratifying in its sheer reductivism, its pure claim to form. (This is design as DNA.) To stop for a moment and grasp that humility is a wake-up call: perhaps, at its core, this is what it means to engage, not through professionalism or elitism or branding, not as a function of clever positioning or even cleverer propaganda, but as a human being, stripped of defenses, devoid of posture, liberated from the vicissitudes of style, the burden of cool. Somewhere in that realization, indelibly connected to the social, intellectual, and spiritual circuitry that governs our moral choices, lies that long-neglected nucleus of mysterious human wonder that is, in fact, the soul.

This is a book about having a conscience, and about doing the right thing. It is not a religious proposition or a righteous oratory, but instead takes a longer view, considering the broader questions that define what it means to be a human being, living with other human beings, contributing to a future that is of our collective making. In an era so massively dominated by technology, it has become far too easy to engage in self-congratulatory monologues rather than to recognize and absorb the larger and arguably more critical (and far more intangible) questions that arise when we stop to contemplate our own ineffable frailties. To be human is to struggle with the unknowable. To design is to make things knowable. It is in the ever-widening gulf separating these two polarities that this book locates itself.

DESIGN IS, ADMITTEDLY, AN INDUSTRY THAT DOES NOT REQUIRE certification. With the possible exception of architecture, the practices that collectively characterize the design professions—graphic design, industrial design, fashion, landscape, textile, interior, and interaction design, among others—do not typically require a license. Which makes everyone a designer.

Or, for that matter, no one.

But that's just a tiny piece of a far more ambiguous puzzle. Professional validation notwithstanding, what makes design mean something? What makes a designed object or experience result in an emotional response or produce a memorable reaction? What is the connection between value and reward, between an enduring memory and an irrevocable act? If design is, by its very nature, such a public form of expression, then how are such idiosyncratic reactions to be anticipated and understood, let alone addressed? At a time when our collective cultural priorities tend to skew toward the fast and furious, design has become a curious commodity. Is it a process or a practice? A product or a platform? And if, arguably, it defies such easy classification, then who wants and needs it, produces and consumes it?

This, in turn, raises critical questions about why we design, what we design, who we design for, and why we do so. Is making things the sum total of what designers truly contribute? Or are aesthetic concerns and production values simply select components within a deeper cultural ecosystem that we have only just begun to penetrate? Increasingly, this is becoming murky territory. As the boundaries between professions become more porous and the defining characteristics of design expand and proliferate, it has never been easier to call yourself a maker. Everyone has a website, a blog, a "brand"— making design as a concept at once more accessible and conceptually less unique. (If everyone's a designer, why hire a designer?) With every new online seller comes more stuff to purchase; with every new commerce-enabled site, more things to covet. True, the basic economics of design depend to a great extent upon such transactions, but we minimize the value of what we do—and who we are—if we restrict ourselves to measuring our achievements primarily in relationship to what we produce.

To be fair, there has been significant recent progress with regard to designers responding to much more complex social needs, applying their knowledge to addressing problems in developing nations, for example, collaborating on bottom-up—or at least sideways—solutions for everything from more affordable lawn mowers to cleaner drinking water. Initiatives that target what might be termed "design for the common good" remind us that design can be a catalyst for change, which explains, to a certain extent, why design has become an increasingly popular theoretical conceit in business. This clearly represents a strategic advantage for designers, though their contributions remain, to a certain degree, sooner relegated to what they make than framed by what they think. Trained designers, concentrating rigorously on the eloquence of form, bring their talents to a broad spectrum of goods and services that both serve and delight us, but it is hard to imagine such contributions counting on a global scale until we require design students to study a second language, or read books outside the design canon, or understand the rudiments of genetics.

And that's just for starters. Indeed—and this may be the biggest shocker yet—design will not matter as long as design education is stalled in the nineteenth-century academic deep-freeze model of the atelier. Though its benefits are numerous (the studio—like the laboratory—is essentially an incubation chamber, and this matters hugely at a developmental level), it remains an antiquated paradigm because it fails to take into consideration the idea that design is a great deal more than the sum of its parts. To privilege skill is to fine-tune the mechanics of making, but it does so at the risk of imprisoning the mind—and, for that matter, the soul—thereby restricting the extent to which design actually can and should matter.

Make no mistake: the studio is ground zero in the sense that the designer requires the space and time and freedom to engage in complex investigations of form; to speculate and iterate; and to gain fluency in the skill sets that remain the formal bedrock of our disciplines. (Technology alone makes this a complex and constantly changing proposition.) But that's only the tip of the iceberg—and it might just be the wrong tip. What if—in addition to our dedication to producing things—we looked inward, instead of out? What if we considered the human values that drive individuals, instead of problem solving for the greater good? What if we started with ourselves, asking ethical questions, moral questions, ruthlessly critical questions?

In the end, design matters because it is an intrinsically humanist discipline, tethered to the very core of why we exist. It frames our conception of power; informs our belief about personal dignity; piques our curiosity about fiction and fantasy; highlights our yearning for beauty and romance; and engages our eternal appetite for narrative. Design matters because it gives form to our past and dimension to our future, but this is not because we sit on nice chairs, or wear pretty shoes, or pride ourselves on our good taste in belts or cars or video games. Design—which traffics in but is not beholden to consumer culture—does not matter because it is hip or hot or cool or cheap or new or rare or bold or sexy, even though these are all qualities that may claim to entice us at any given moment, for reasons that have everything to do with who we are, not what we own. Design—which is grounded in mathematical certainties, relying upon composition and orchestration, on gesture and nuance—does not matter because it is pleasing to the eye, even though we applaud its beauty and its purpose and its presence in our lives. Design matters because of the why, not the what; the sentiment, not the acquisition. Design matters because people matter, and the purpose of this book is to examine precisely this proposition: to consider the conscience-driven rules of human engagement within which design must operate. This is a book about design as it relates to human beings. Because that is what matters most of all.

Chapter One: Authority

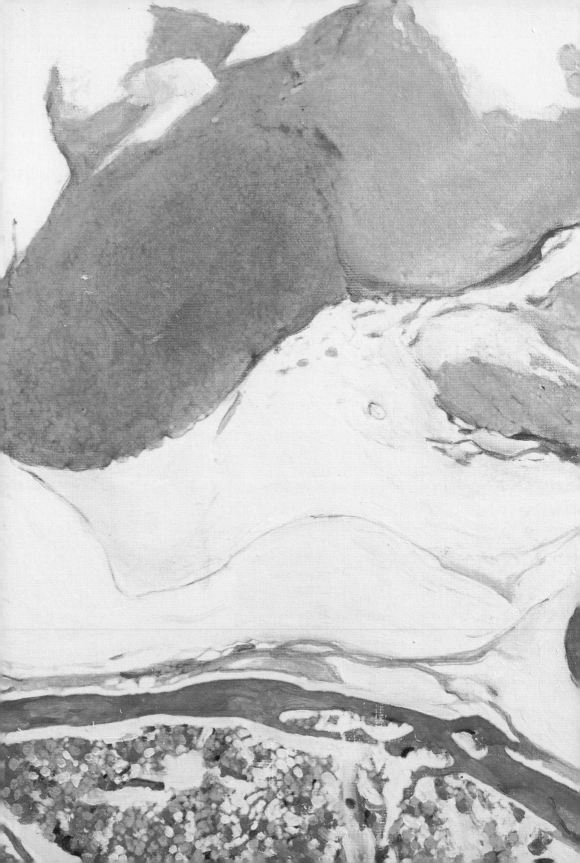

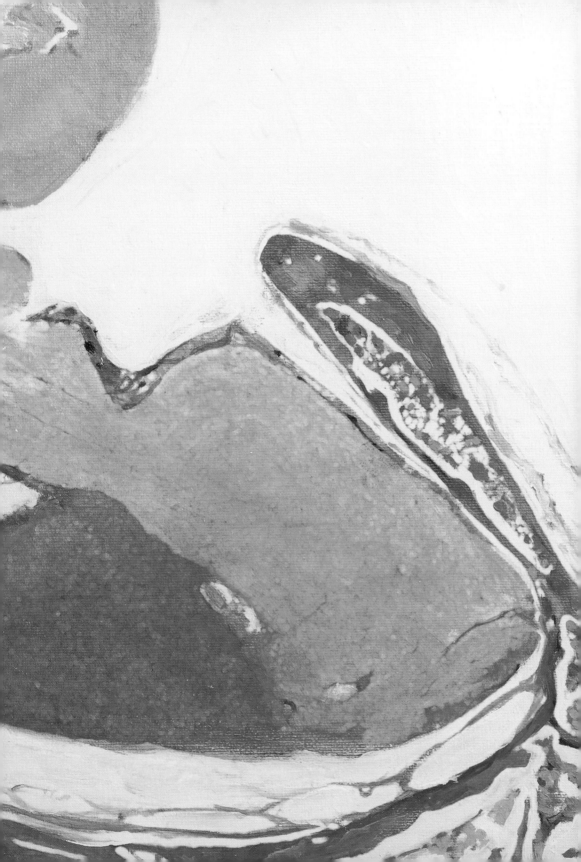

RECENTLY, THE NIGHT BEFORE AN EARLY FLIGHT FROM LONDON TO New York, I checked into my flight online. Due to the lateness of the hour, my hotel's business office was locked; the only option, it seemed, was to have my boarding pass delivered to me electronically, which I dutifully proceeded to do. I arrived at the airport early the next morning to the sudden realization that I had no Internet connection: by conjecture, I had no ticket. Without the physical document in evidence, I needed another way to prove that my booking was legitimate—that I was, in fact, legitimate. This turned out to be a rather labor-intensive process, fueled in no small measure by the exigencies of modern airport security, and made arguably worse by the scarcity of caffeine at that early hour. Was I the same person who had checked in online only hours earlier? Tethered to an airline kiosk, I methodically answered a number of questions that quelled any suspicions about my true identity— which, once verified, produced the desired boarding pass.

This is a common scenario for anyone attempting to reconcile the digital with the actual. If expedience favors the former, reality privileges the tangible thing itself: the original, accept-no-imitations document. From passports to licenses, receipts to diplomas, birth certificates to tax forms to pay stubs, human beings both crave and depend upon validation in the form of tangible, visual authority. Paradoxical as it may seem, we have come to value such forms of authority perhaps because our digital lives remain so intangible. Unlike a file that can be corrupted or a system that can be hacked, an original document is, by its very nature, a unique artifact requiring vigilant protection. (Given the ubiquity of copy machines and scanners, duplication is an effortless task: by conjecture, so is proliferation and, not surprisingly, identity theft.) Digital exchanges have their own visual protocols and cues that help us decode the passage of time, protect by password, even register the ongoing participation of others. With each subsequent e-mail, the color of an original message changes. Retweets are buttressed by hashtags; crowd-pleasing posts are boosted by thumbs-up emoticons. (The limitations of "liking"—and they are legend—will be explored in a subsequent chapter.) With each "share" the value of the original is fundamentally diminished, even as we applaud its fleeting popularity. (Could there be any better example of planned obsolescence than the dubious tag, "trending"?) Yet while such participatory gestures go a long way toward cementing community and reinforcing belonging, they also effectively deplete our basic sense of trust. In an age in which we "fast-track" through airports and "one-click" through websites, proof by paper may, ironically, be more powerful than ever.

Online, unarmed by such material examples of legitimacy, we must identify and ultimately defend ourselves by passwords. Here, the very presumption that one's virtual peregrinations can be sheltered by code is itself a questionable maneuver: it's protection by proxy, a shaky proposition— particularly if you fail to make note of your latest username/password combo. Coordinating passwords alone can prove a soul-crushing exercise, involving strategy and secrecy and, for some of us, no shortage of despair. An erroneous entry is an instant reminder of your failure to be who you say you are, and forgotten password prompts are even worse. Name of your favorite stuffed animal when you were four years old? Top outfielder for the Brooklyn Dodgers in 1937? Case-sensitive, alphanumeric, fifteen digits of cAsEsEnSiTiVe anagrams—does it really matter? The deeper you go, the more powerless you become, and frustration only results in soaring blood pressure. (Or worse, a temporary lockout.) Make no mistake: digital expedience may favor the modern multitasker, but the forgotten password quickly becomes its own miserable circle of hell.

To date, certain forms of visual documentation have successfully resisted the lure of digitization, and of these the passport is perhaps unique. Although reduced to a kind of robotic shorthand—our metrics are, after all, intended to synchronize within a larger network of global nations and their respective endpoints at border control—the civilian's experience of carrying a passport remains undeniably analog. Passports are totems of no-nonsense specificity, containers of particularity, and, outside of DNA samples, perhaps our most universally legitimate calling cards. When we travel outside our home countries, we are shadowed by what the world acknowledges to be a kind of preordained set of metrics: at once numerical and descriptive, they're pure proof, undeniable evidence that testifies to your true identity. You can't lie about your age on a passport, or fake your looks, or pretend you live in a penthouse at the Ritz (unless you do, but even then you need a passport to prove it).

Since about 1915, American and European passport bearers have been required to submit to the great ignominy of obligatory portraiture. Here, as in the case of the driver's license or the ID card, lies the flattened, forlorn likeness, the mugshot sliced into regulation size and accompanied by the sorts of coordinated metrics—age, height, nationality, and so on—framing the bits and pieces that collectively beget the homogenized identity of the weary tourist. Back then, in those comparatively early days of border etiquette, travelers were also expected to verbally describe their physical qualities: height and hair, face shape and eye color, noses and mouths and complexions. Such information tends, by its very nature, to be characterized by its appeal to brevity (this is, after all, serious one-word-answer territory, facts best delivered without innuendo), none of which deterred the poet

Ezra Pound. His 1926 passport includes a description of his hair color ("fair") and profession ("poet"). But when asked to describe the shape of his chin, he deviated from the perfunctory, choosing a word he believed captured this particular feature with greater zeal: "imperial."

Reviewing historical examples of official documentation—passports, licenses, membership cards, and so on—offers a fascinating lens on social history, material evidence of what mattered and what it looked like when it did. There are forgotten addresses, loopy signatures, telephone numbers with long-defunct exchanges, Christian names redolent of another era, the random markings of identity-specific inky fingerprints. Professions, too, suggest sociological markers of a certain kind (back then, a person might self-identify as a "laborer" or a "ladies maid"), as do the portraits of so many involuntary subjects, stiffly posing in what we once referred to as our Sunday best. The graphic history of calling cards alone illuminates the degree to which design played a profound role in visual authority over time: floral typography, stiff card stock, staged photography—all reflective of a carefully coded social capital. A nineteenth-century woman of position, for instance, would never have included her address on her calling card, lest she be considered too "available." Less may have been more, but it was elegantly embellished through the most decorative of letterforms: women used feminine fonts, while the gentlemanly block letter was typically reserved for, well, gentlemen.

That these documents have come to represent us is, by now, a foregone conclusion. (That so few of us have what might be characterized as an imperial chin is perhaps equally conclusive.) Still, most of us would resist the notion that we are defined by such comparatively broad strokes, particularly in an age marked by heightened electronic consumption. What does it say about the human race if even now, in an age in which the printed word is believed to be imperiled, such fundamental, if ultimately ephemeral, power persists?

This hasn't stopped e-commerce from maturing into a sophisticated system that enables smooth financial transactions allegedly ensuring buyer anonymity. (Strange, too, that anonymity should factor so indelibly into our understanding of authority.) Yet online, customer ratings operate as a kind of turnstile of trust. Your money may not lie in a safe deposit box backed by a Wells Fargo guarantee, but a posse of like-minded shoppers has provided a reliable benchmark for you to evaluate comparative worth before PayPalling. This relationship between the group and the individual—between the collective conscious and one's own God-given right to choose anything (whether it is a book or a blender does not really matter)—is now commonly referred to as "crowdsourcing" and has become a key determinator in all kinds of online activity, a good deal of which is based on visual taste, which is to say subjective opinion. At its best, it's citizen journalism, a fair and leveled playing field where critics are no longer elite practitioners but present, instead, as deeply engaged participants. At its worst, it assumes an artificially democratic utopia of stunning sameness where we share equally in opinions, desires, and needs. But do we?

Here is, perhaps, one place where design matters, and where, moreover, it becomes a key differentiator. If something looks better, will more people buy it? If something looks expensive, will more people value it? Inevitably, the role that design plays within the realm of individual taste remains deeply unpredictable: after all, one person's blender of choice may be another person's blight on humanity. A prospective consumer might become swayed by the color of an object, mesmerized by the way it is photographed, or lured by the mere presentation of product or tool or service. Conversely, another person might be put off by the commerciality or deterred by a product's clunky presentation or a site's slow upload speeds. Just as we think about the visual authority by which we self-identify, so too do we consider the design of things when trying to understand what we need and what we want, none of which can be acquired without, well, money. And that has to be designed, too.

AT ONCE A FEAT OF ENGINEERING AND A PHENOMENON OF VISUAL orchestration, the design of currency depends upon a methodology that combines careful anti-counterfeiting measures with a kind of basic legibility: somewhere in there, too, is a basic appeal to beauty. Like postage stamps and stock certificates, there's a kind of majesty to money—borrowing from the likenesses of world leaders, drawing from the significance of key historical events or the presumed recognizability of key cultural symbols, money in general (and banknotes in particular) are visual authority writ large. And while there are now acknowledged standards for "best practices" in the design and distribution of web-based venues for electronic commerce—from password-protected shopping carts to offline verification by SMS (shorthand for Short Message Service)—real money still pulls rank because its visual authority lies, at least as of this writing, safely beyond the realm of interpersonal production. Of course, now that three-dimensional printers can generate everything from food to guns to body parts, the production of coins (not to mention paper currency) sits squarely within the realm of the possible. The interrogation of our assumptions about what constitutes ethical decision making lies at the core of this debate. Authority—once defined as the power to enforce obedience—exists as a deeply human prerogative long before it presents as a commodity. Is it design that invests something with meaning and value, or the designer?

All of this, in turn, raises intriguing questions about ATM interfaces, which are governed by all sorts of protocols, many—though not all—of which have as much to do with visual thinking as they do the vernacular specifics of the country in which they reside. (That people need money is universal; how they choose to view and access it, perhaps less so.) The issues that drive and determine the needs of user interface protocols in general, and of so-called "human-centered" design in particular, are significant (and well beyond the purview of this book), but it would not be an oversimplification to suggest that where money is considered, authority—yes, ours, over our own money—is thought to be in everyone's best interest, and where the automation of online transactions is concerned, the degree of success or failure of such authority hinges on an implied trust that must, at its very core, reside in something visual. Beyond the promises of coded safety and password protocols, how to anticipate and calibrate this kind of trust is very much the role of branding, which relies as much upon psychology (what does a given audience want?) as it does form (what does that thing they want look like)?

And here is where things begin to get really interesting.

The celebrated American designer Paul Rand confessed that he once chose a particular shade of blue for a client because it so closely resembled the signature color of the legendary jeweler Tiffany's. The idea that exalted value could be subconsciously transferred by the association of something as seemingly ubiquitous as a mere color struck him as spectacularly clever, and indeed it was. In this instance, authority was not conveyed by jumping through the hoops required to ensure safety (and by conjecture, establishing value) but was instead delivered seamlessly through the sheer power of suggestion. Such deft delivery of something as specific as credibility through color illuminates the degree to which visual authority is as much a science as an art, benefiting at every turn from a tacit engagement with the idea of the psychological cue, or trigger. Frankly, this explains a lot. If visual triggers were not emotional triggers, nobody would go to the movies. There would be significantly less buyer's remorse, no online dating industry, and virtually no through-the-roof sales for the annual *Sports Illustrated* swimsuit issue.

The idea that visual authority has an impact on economics may not be so surprising, then: in contemporary culture we place an enormous premium on things that look good, and things that look good cost money. So we convince ourselves we are worthy, realism is trumped by optimism, and the aspirational self triumphs: want becomes need, need becomes greed, and the visual cycle of supply and demand shifts into high gear. But now there is a new element in play, and that is the degree to which we can—and do—insinuate ourselves into the equation. This has everything to do with technology and the newly minted reach of social media, and is perhaps especially tricky with regard to photography. And here, the impact of readily accessible pictures introduces a slippery slope all its own.

To the extent that pictures speak louder than words, a simple image can elevate (or torpedo) the authority of almost anything. Personal metrics drive the sales data of everything from art to books to cars online, which is all well and good, except that somewhere along the line we've unwittingly entered into a kind of commodification brokerage with the persistent broadcasting of our own psyches. Picture-driven social sites like Instagram and dating sites like Tinder use images as currency, with tags and likes and yes/no swipes driving distribution, and it is this, more than anything else, that raises new questions about the misguided degree to which we've ceded control over the sorts of essential personal values that once guided us. Consider the frequency with which young girls, for instance, are said to be using social media to "poll" their friends and acquaintances about their looks, and then ask yourself: at what point did we begin to teach our children to reach outwardly for public reinforcement in order to solidify their sense of self? In this view, the entire notion of what constitutes visual authority shifts from an external set of vetted coordinates framed by a random assortment of inanimate documents to a deeply human set of personal, emotional, and more mindful conceits, cloaked in effortless, push-button capabilities. In a sadly ironic modern-day twist on the classic Cartesian notion of selfhood, we post, therefore we are.

Sadder still, what was implicit in Descartes's famous proclamation was the idea of time: time spent reflecting inwardly, contemplating an idea before acting upon it. Perhaps we have come to depend so much upon external totems of validation because we no longer trust that inward, if largely invisible, voice. Perhaps, too, this reinforces the degree to which we trust the simulacra more than the self, elevating those banal emblems of visual reinforcement—the tickets and diplomas and other examples of external authority—because they are one-offs, notarized and official and impervious to the more informal, self-generated artifacts that now loosely circumscribe our daily online orbits. We thus place exalted value on precisely that which we cannot personally produce, because in spite of grooming ourselves to be autodidacts and publishers and proselytizers, in spite of our capacity to pimp and promote and spin, we still crave proof: proof of ownership and authorship and citizenship, proof in the form of physical, palpable, and indelible documentation. In the end, whether or not your chin is imperial is not really the issue. Actually remembering to bring your boarding pass, on the other hand, may well be.

Chapter Two: Fantasy

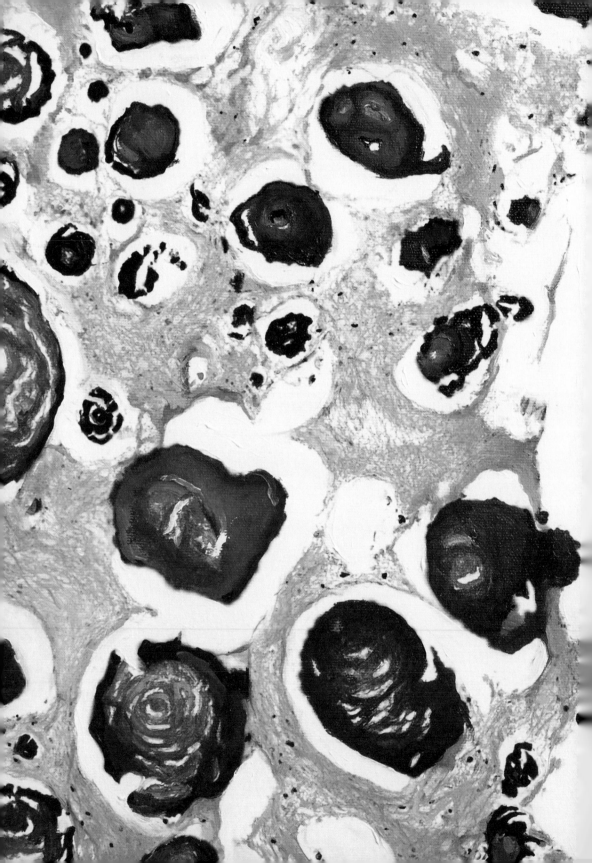

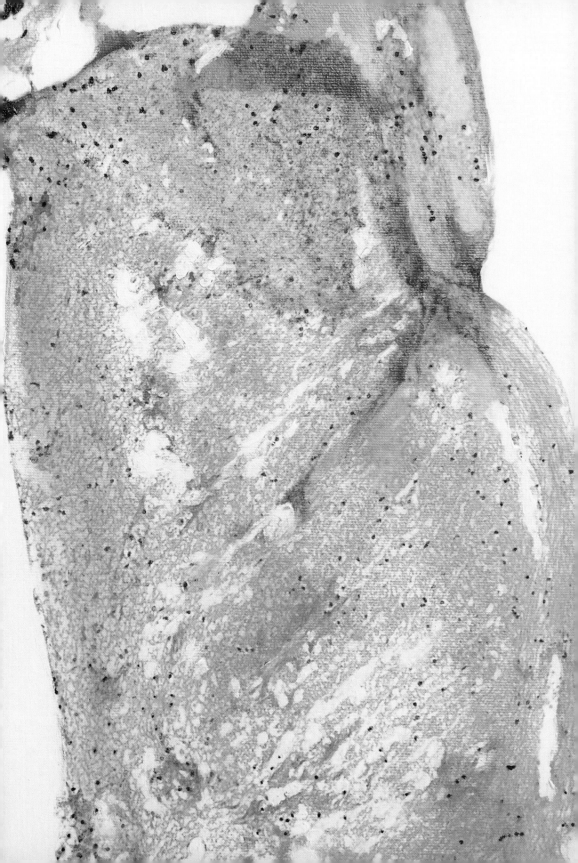

FOR SEVERAL YEARS, AN ACQUAINTANCE OF MINE, AN ARCHITECT, hosted a regular New Year's Eve ritual whereupon his unsuspecting guests were met with a particular design challenge. At each place setting in his dining room lay a band of pliable cardboard. Below, in his basement, sat a table garnished with no shortage of objects—newspapers and magazines, scissors and glue, trash and treasure generously distributed across the room. During the evening, each guest was invited to partake of this visual buffet, choosing at will those elements which each felt best captured their hopes for the coming year. At midnight the assembled guests would share (and wear) these "crowns of aspiration," as they came to be called, thus ringing in the New Year with fantasy-driven evocations of imagination, humor, and hope.

A fantasy can perform as a parable or a fetish, a wishful motivator or a compulsive trap. This explains the persistence of rags to riches as a theme (think *Oliver Twist*) and a meme (think *Who Wants to Be a Millionaire*), but it also suggests that the relationship between the visual thing and its "fantastical" reading hinges on the ways we both digest and disseminate stories themselves. To a child, "what if" scenarios are the backbone of the fairy tale (what if I grow up to be a princess?), while to a visual thinker, such speculation lies at the core of the design process itself (what if this were bigger or bluer, smaller or stronger?). Each relies upon the power of fantasy to break free of normative patterns. Each grows from a dream.

It has long been believed that there is a fundamentally human need to have a dream life. It's why we have fables and fairy tales, where the stories we both tell and hear—wishful and fanciful, if by their very nature apocryphal—endure precisely because they appeal to a fundamental human appetite for wonder and mystery, illusion and fantasy. At the same time, they feed our craving for a kind of moral certainty, an established bank of truths. That certain stories are rooted in ancient myth not only enhances their primal power but also homogenizes their impact by assuming we are all easily reducible to certain basic hopes and dreams. Reinforced by everything from biblical parables to blockbuster movies, these classic paradigms root themselves in our collective cultural consciousness: our heroes may change, but the fundamental tales—or, for that matter, the iconic images that represent them—do not, and soon yesterday's steel (baron) is today's silicon (valley entrepreneur).

Fables are the apotheosis of fantasies because they are so didactic and binary, equation-like in their predictability and deeply satisfying as a result. At the high end, such fantasies ennoble us: behave honorably and be canonized. At the low and arguably more visual end, such fantasies degrade us: this is porn territory (where the external fantasy can be harnessed and sold), but it extends, in a general sense, to such things as conspicuous consumption, celebrity worship, and mindlessly renewable greed. (The degree to which these sorts of fantasies are endlessly repeatable testifies, if nothing else, to their banality.) At its core, all storytelling is perhaps a form of fantasy, piquing the senses, provoking the mind, feeding the imagination. In many European languages, including but not limited to Italian, German, and French, the word for imagination is, in fact, fantasy.

The relative success of storytelling lies partly in the story and partly in the telling. While clearly subject to the nuances and cadences of the writer or raconteur, a story instantly takes root as a set of fleeting images conjured in the mind of the listener. Yet as much as fantasy can be engaged through language—"These were thick silk stockings," writes D. H. Lawrence in *Women in Love,* "vermilion, cornflower blue, and grey, bought in Paris..."—it is the pictorial cue that sears an indelible image into your memory, where it lingers and endures. Compare Lawrence's highly visual prose with the iconic scene in *The Graduate* where Anne Bancroft, in the role of Mrs. Robinson, slowly removes her nylons, and you begin to realize how the inexhaustible potency of pictures trumps even the most compellingly written narrative.

But fantasy is a puzzle, one that we often, if unwittingly, try to reengineer in our own minds, which may explain in part how we experience the visual. Consider, for example, the lure of pictorial real estate: here we mentally "complete" the picture, imagining ourselves in environments that do not belong to us, engaging in a kind of casual and highly aspirational fiction. The threshold separating the picture from the person (namely, you) is effectively a porous one. All it takes is focus. (And funds: you can't be Mrs. Robinson, but you might be able to buy a house like hers.) Motivated by practicalities like budget and location, the dedicated home seeker browses images of possible options, only to be instantly catapulted into playfully speculative scenarios that may have little if anything to do with practical considerations including location, layout, or budget. To look at photographs in the window of a realtor—or, for that matter, through any of a number of highly visual online destinations—is to instantly imagine yourself living a completely different life. You fantasize mindlessly, seeing yourself framed by overstuffed chairs, awash in sun-drenched rooms, and surrounded by deliriously healthy and happy pets. No matter that you have never been able to keep even the smallest cactus plant alive: here, in the wishful wonderland of image-driven real estate, the world really *can* be yours.

At a more modest, if insidious, level, the unsolicited furniture catalog activates a similar fantasy. Once, such publications were a prime locus for a particularly gendered kind of leisure activity: nineteenth-century women not only sourced home furnishings in catalogs but often reserved them afterward for their daughters, encouraging them to cut them up and "play house," thereby experimenting with the sorts of domestic skills they would one day be expected to inherit. Today these volumes—thick magazines promoting IKEA modernism, Restoration Hardware classicism, and everything in between—rely upon a series of preordained formal taxonomies. Room by room, season after season, they arrive unsolicited, seeking to anticipate the imagined needs of a broadly presumed demographic. As containers of the material, furniture catalogs serve as highly indexical systems for domestic order: organized and useful, informative and clear. But as staged mini-utopias, they're pure fiction, subtle in their visual innuendo, sly in their psychological pull. On some primal level, we participate within these artfully manufactured scenarios by unwittingly insinuating ourselves into and onto them. The ensuing, if silent, psychological dynamic goes something like this: if I buy this chair, I will be happy. The desired artifact thus becomes a physical extension of what is essentially a tiered pantomime of imagined acquisition: consumption as conspicuous, design as prosthetic. In this context the designed thing becomes its own crown of aspiration, a wishful material extension of ourselves—a trinket, a tool, an appendage.

Material culture is awash in such seductions, and we are, all of us, subject to such tantalizing visual lures. Taste notwithstanding, is this not the role of advertising, the appeal of fashion? "If you work in fashion," observes the French shoe designer Christian Louboutin, "you have to give people fantasy." Italian shoe designer Manolo Blahnik concurs. "About half my designs are controlled fantasy," he notes. "Fifteen percent are total madness, and the rest are bread-and-butter designs." And what is wrong with that? Bread is to butter as clothing is to fashion as shelter is to architecture: each fulfills a basic human need. If that were the end of the story, man would indeed live by bread alone, all of us dressing in identical sacks and dwelling in parallel huts. This is where design, as a discipline, surfaces as a skilled differentiator—providing alternatives, feeding dreams, addressing our requirement for function while gesturing to our ever-present appetite for fantasy. Because that's a basic human need, too.

To crave an alluring item is to imagine yourself owning it, and the relationship between acquisition and contentment, improbable as it may seem, is very real. Yet the ethics surrounding how we justify—let alone reward—such cravings remain startlingly unclear. Designers make things that people want and need, sourcing materials and refining ideas, ideally in a manner that makes a positive contribution to the planet. (First: do no harm.) Yet however responsibly sourced, ergonomically crafted, and mindfully distributed, that responsibility is not individually tracked, nor does it extend in most cases beyond the receiving line. A designer might design a typeface for public distribution, but that does not prevent a guerrilla army from adopting it for their own nefarious uses. An architect can design a lean and sustainable, LEED-certified house, but that doesn't ensure that its future owners will compost or recycle or furnish it with locally harvested wood. And a fashion designer might engage the most perfectly exquisite supermodels to showcase her clothes, but that does not stop the rest of us nonsupermodels from purchasing and posing in them. In other words, the designer's fantasy is not now, nor has it ever been, the same as the consumer's.

If beauty is in the eye of the beholder, fantasy is not far behind, and predicting what people crave is a tempting if impossible task. (This is the work of trend forecasters, branding strategists, and retailers all over the world.) Conceptually, to imagine yourself, say, owning the coveted thing—whether it is a penthouse or a pepper shaker does not really matter— is to convince yourself that possession is tantamount to contentment, a harmless exercise. But the thing about desire is that it breeds more desire. This explains, at least in part, the recursive loop known as conspicuous consumption, and it points out the degree to which design in general, and fantasy in particular, inevitably fuels it. That line—between want and need, function and fantasy—is a tricky one.

Many years ago, when all telephones required landlines (and long before they were considered "smart"), we occasionally employed other people to take messages. At first there were switchboard operators—long rows of people (women, mostly) weaving connectivity across perforated walls, one plug at a time. Later there would be answering services, a random turnstile of anonymous receptionists ferrying calls and shepherding messages for anyone too busy to stay at home waiting for the phone to ring. Answering services were cultural oddities: you paid monthly for a real person at the other end of a line who recorded all your phone messages until you had the time to retrieve them yourself, which you did by dialing in with a mailbox code. Once the code was accessed, you spoke to an actual person—a faceless, nameless human being, who soon came to know the most intimate details about you: your fight with your mother, your latest flirtation, your annoying boss. Answering services were captivating repositories of data and drama, their employees the anonymous keepers of your deeply held secrets, keenly monitoring your evolving social narrative. Though staffers were essentially discreet, you couldn't help but feel somewhat unsettled about the extent of their knowledge. And there was nothing so appallingly shame-inducing as calling in expectantly, only to find that no one was currently trying to reach you. (I engaged such a service briefly in the late 1980s, so I would know.)

Thomas Edison once referred to the telephone as an invention that annihilated time and space, "bringing the human family in closer touch." As a prognostication for the portable freedoms of the future, he couldn't have been further from the truth. (Today our phones may be smart, but they're hardly conduits for closeness.) But the introduction of answering machines— now nearly half a century ago—represented a significant paradigm shift with regard to personal scheduling and time management, simply by introducing a recording device that eliminated the tether connecting you to your desk, and thereby liberating you from a kind of onerous, if involuntary, house arrest. With an answering machine, a new kind of self-actualized fantasy was now actionable, because it allowed for endless posturing. You could be at home screening your calls, pretending not to be at home. You could get a friend to record your outgoing message in a silly voice. You could duck, wax poetic, or call in sick without a GPS tag to smoke you out. Big and clunky, retrofitted with plastic cassettes and thick power cords, answering machines were social media before the phrase ever existed.

The first answering machines debuted in 1960 but did not become commercially available until the advent of digital technologies—nearly twenty-five years later—delivering radical independence to anyone with a landline. But they also led to new physical and material needs: more outlets, larger tables for telephones, the invention of power strips and surge suppressors. The advent of videocassette recorders did the same for televisions, and with the introduction of laptops came something called "peripherals"—an entire new subindustry of cases and containers and cords, plus all the contraptions you needed for transporting them. Such innovations gave all of us a longer leash (no longer did you need to stay at home to wait for a phone call or watch something on television), which, curiously, showed us that it was the experience provided by the object that fueled the fantasy of freedom, not the object itself. Not yet. Not until the iPhone.

The iPhone changed the conversation about both the object (beautiful, magical) and the experience (practical, portable) by merging tasks with entertainment, work with fun. Small and slender, shiny and sleek, never was less so very much more. But even more than its pure power as an object of desire was its transformative role in the realignment of so many previously disparate behaviors. Over the course of a few short years, the iPhone changed the way we took pictures, had conversations, paid bills, listened to music, commuted to work, navigated the world, and played games—and it is this perhaps more than anything that has reinvigorated our willingness to engage in fantasy, reminding us that on some fundamental level, all fantasy is a kind of play. It relaxes the mind, recalibrates the eye, and reminds us that, at heart, we are all about six years old. Oliver Wendell Holmes understood this implicitly. "Men do not quit playing because they grow old," he wrote. "They grow old because they quit playing."

The relationship between design and play was a subject of considerable interest to certain postwar modernists including (but not limited to) Paul Rand, Shigeo Fukuda, Herbert Matter, and Ladislav Sutnar, design practitioners who hailed from four different countries yet shared a consuming interest in the relationship between variables and constants, structure and freedom. Their work demonstrated in strikingly different ways the degree to which playfulness is, perhaps more than anything, a function of constraints. Taking their cues from the parameters of classic game playing (if not game theory) itself, they noted that certain binary conditions are key regulators in most games, supporting the physical elements that in turn make games possible: from the equilateral sides of the game board (which presuppose an identical measure of real estate for all players) to the centrally located net on a tennis court, "play" is what happens once certain formal boundaries are established.

Originally published in 1965, Paul Rand's now famous essay "Design and the Play Instinct" traced the notion of play as far back as the Greeks, and made a particular case for the importance of such thinking in design education. For Rand, producing work in the spirit of play had to do with such basic elements as harmony, balance, and composition, the hand-drawn gesture against the manufactured one. For the Japanese designer Shigeo Fukuda, play was about illusion—optical, comical, perceptual; it was all about puzzles and mystery, humor, and satire; about the striking power of visual elusiveness. In the case of the Swiss-born Matter, it revealed itself in dynamic shifts of image and scale, leading to surprising yet simple juxtapositions. For the Czech-born polymath Sutnar, it was about the interplay of form and space, geometry and delight, which was evident not only in the end products but equally in the hands-on process that led to their fruition: the mechanical.

At its core, the now defunct mechanical or "paste-up" was a map for the printer, indicating crop marks and color breaks, silhouettes and screens, with detailed tissue sketches upon layers of acetate onto which type would be waxed into position. Ultimately, each of these diaphanous layers of segregated content would be sandwiched together and taped onto a piece of illustration board, a procedural blueprint for the final printed piece. But if printers depended upon mechanicals to represent factual evidence, designers (and the clients they served) depended equally upon their ability to simulate a final form: they hinted at what *might* be—not only what would be.

Because they were hand-rendered, mechanicals retained the unbridled energy of their maker: they could be loose and gestural; disciplined and reserved; or amplified with detailed shading and contouring—each of these a tease, a masterful allusion to the shape of things to come. In Sutnar's exquisite and complex mechanicals, type is "greeked" (classic shorthand for the controlled scribbling meant to simulate typography) with precision and purpose. Fields of color—Rubyliths, Amberliths—jockeyed for position with benday dots and tissue overlays, often flagged with cryptic subtexts and mindfully scripted notes. To understand these mechanicals today requires a kind of conceptual leap of faith: they're at once an imagined archaeological excavation and a deep dive into design history—in viewing them, you find yourself mentally reconstructing the composite layers to approximate what was intended to be the final product. They're precise and prescriptive, but because they take something two-dimensional and point to so much more, and because they reveal the traces of human gesture, there's something magically transcendent about them. Mechanicals like Sutnar's are playful and purposeful at the same time, redolent in their layers, loving evocations of one man's aspirational vision. A mechanical might be a vehicle for intention, but in Sutnar's hands they were pure flights of fancy.

Design, by its very nature, is a practical art with a public focus, but that doesn't mean that it too does not benefit from the what-if scenarios made so much more tangible by the integration of hand and eye, hand and object, hand and heart. To review Sutnar's extraordinarily robust body of design work is not only to witness the material evidence of a big, restless talent: it's a reminder that the best way to grow as a maker is to keep on making things, to look closely, to think objectively, to imagine fiercely. ("Knowledge is limited to all we now know and understand," Einstein once wrote, "while imagination embraces the entire world, and all there ever will be to know and understand.") Designers know it is their duty to map the future, to invent and make things we need, things we can use. But along the way, we are reminded that the process is as valuable as the product, the method as potentially revelatory as the motive. In the end, we dream because we can.

Chapter Three: Identity

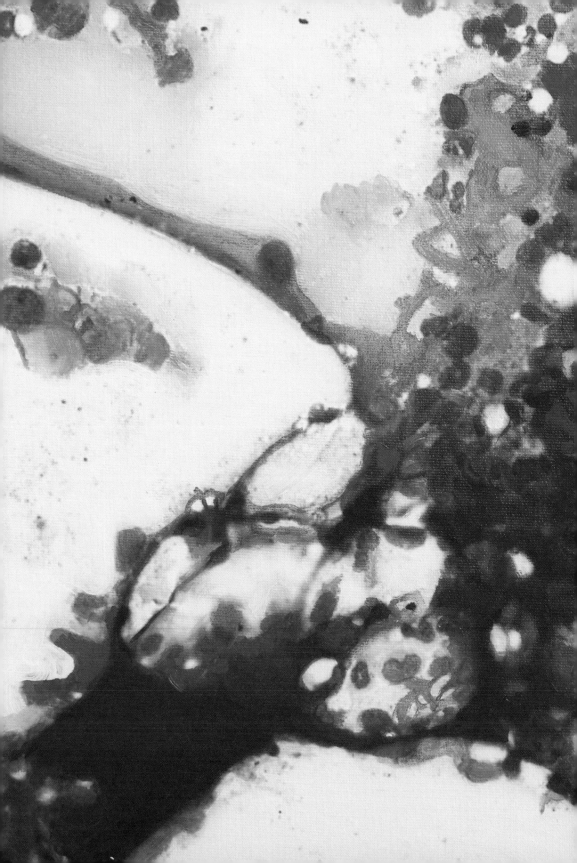

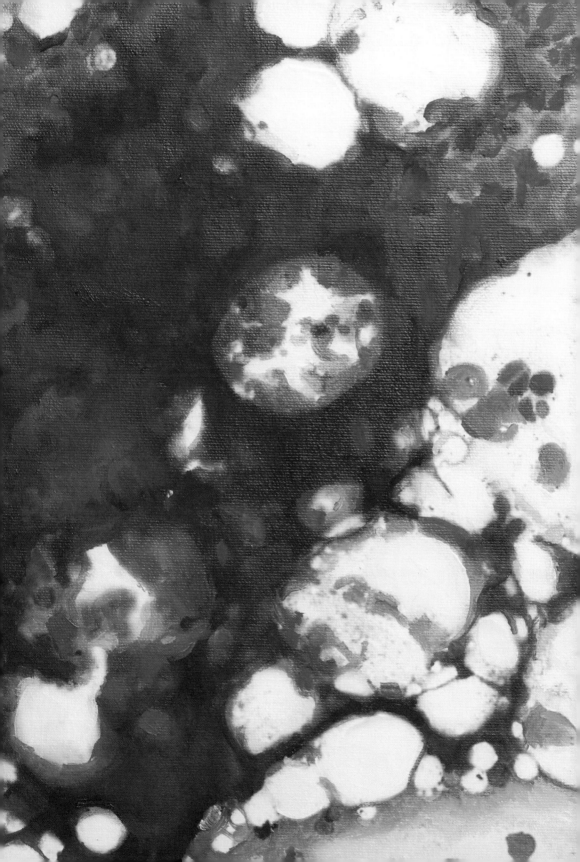

IN THE SPRING OF 2014 A DEEPLY TROUBLED COLLEGE STUDENT WENT on a shooting rampage at the University of California at Santa Barbara, killing half a dozen innocent people before taking his own life. In the days and weeks that followed, journalists began to piece together the killer's backstory: they interviewed his family, traced his activities, and gradually began to reverse engineer the psychological tapestry of one man's profoundly fractured psyche, in an effort to try and reconstitute who in fact he really was.

At the core of this highly publicized inquiry lay his social media profile— his rants were meticulously self-documented, captured on video and posted with enormous precision and care—that collectively provided a mesmerizing, if terrifying, visual snapshot of his distributed online presence. This is not, in fact, so surprising: such forensic research is standard practice in most homicide investigations, and in many ways this case was no different. What *is* significant is the degree to which it has come to be the new normal: today personal identity manifests as an increasingly kinetic kit of parts, changeable and disenfranchised visual components that randomly tell others where and what—and, more troublingly, *who* we are. To "read" social media is to assume an essential visual literacy in this perpetually kinetic, public space. The target keeps moving: identity, once fixed, is now a function of dynamic acts of visual and perceptual displacement.

While products and businesses rely upon visible brand recognition, human beings subscribe to a different notion, reserving the right to project messages that might, in fact, be contradictory. And here's where it gets tricky: if human identity is fixed (DNA doesn't lie) and visual identity is focused (a trademark is a trademark), then why are the visual evocations of human identity so infinitely varied? And why, on the screen-based venues where they typically proliferate, are they ultimately so uninteresting?

The answer may lie in the feed itself—that constant stream of perpetually unfolding "news," catering to the impatience we bring to this medium (which is, somewhat paradoxically, its most enduring characteristic). This is, arguably, the greatest lure of social media: on the Internet, you can be anything you want to be. A gastroenterologist who grows exotic orchids. A trilingual dog trainer. A political pundit with an encyclopedic knowledge of wine. Or none of these. (Or, for that matter, all of them.) Because the platforms themselves are fairly streamlined, you are neither encouraged nor rewarded for your devotion to consistency. Yes, you might elect to methodically document your breakfast every day for a year, but given that you are the star of your own visual autobiography, who really cares? One of the most addictive aspects of social media is its essentially libertarian disregard for quality control—this is where you can simply go rogue and try on different personalities for size— which may explain its stunning popularity among that not insignificant portion of the population known as teenagers, raised on a diet of multiple choice, the screen's—indeed, the Internet's—most enduring legacy.

To spend any amount of time actually "managing" one's online profile is to become an instant curator: you are, after all, the one in charge of shaping the version of yourself you want others to see. It is a formidable task, of course, for anyone concerned with their public image, which, in the old days, was the domain of public relations firms but now engages virtually anyone with an e-mail address. From there it's a quick jump to Pinterest and WordPress and Facebook and Flickr, Snapchat and Stampsy and Tumblr and Twitter,

LinkedIn and Instagram and Donder and Blitzen. Well, maybe not those last two. Not yet, anyway.

Some years back, network behemoth America Online introduced a reduced monthly family plan that allowed up to five subscribers to share a single account, only to notice a demonstrable uptick in users with multiple personality disorder. More recently, social media platforms like Facebook have come to allow tiered privacy settings and selective sharing, while picture-based sites like Flickr and Pinterest permit multiple albums and parsed (even private) collections. Unlike the days of modernist restraint when less was more, more is now more, much more, more than more, because it keeps proliferating endlessly, obstreperously. And thanks to the clever indexical practice known as "tagging," it's all better organized, too. That said, the magic of finding anonymous, unidentified photographs may soon go the way of dinosaurs: with tagging in place, the culture of vernacular photography will likely not survive this century.

The process of tagging, however, offers only a partial solution. On a mechanical level, managing your virtual footprint takes time and care. Financially, to have more (space, access to space) costs more. And submitting to the organizational standards of public media platforms essentially shoehorns everyone into, well, if not the same box, then at least a similarly *shaped* box. Curiously, we rarely think to challenge this subtly enforced sameness. We don't resist the fact that our e-mails are often written in the same typeface, that our Twitter feeds are all the same length, or that participation in these comparatively new public arenas has obliged us to fit in visually according to criteria not of our own making: indeed, that have nothing to do with who we truly are or perhaps even who we want to be. The "shape" our public pronouncements take mirrors the formal taxonomies of the platforms themselves. In so doing, we're all obliged to share the same visual grammar: the posts and hashtags, the lengths of our tweets, the limitations of our Vine videos, and so forth. Had the utopian promises of certain planned postwar communities like Levittown expanded to overtake the entire continent, many (most?) of us might have complained. (Viewed in context, and seen against the comparatively poor conditions of early twentieth-century urban overcrowding, its then pioneering inhabitants understandably rejoiced.) Conversely, when it comes to today's social media platforms—which, by their very nature, gather us all through a kind of basic, homogenized visual armature—we don't appear to mind in the least.

To a certain extent, the success of any design endeavor lies in a kind of balanced tension between that which is variable and that which is constant. Consider the newspaper, for example: the typeface and grid are fixed, while the news content and photography are variable. Or blue jeans: successful brands lure consumers with a fixed level of quality and a recognizable set of visual cues—the red tag on Levi's back pockets, for instance—while the collections of clothes themselves vary over time. In the case of certain tightly formatted media platforms like Facebook, what changes is how we choose to curate our identities: through pictures and posts, sharing and even snark, each choice contributing to the larger pursuit that telegraphs who we are to our "friends," and of these, pictures are key. At the core of that operation is the "selfie"—the digital, speedy, off-the-cuff self-portrait that has come to represent that minute-by-minute visual chronicle we transmit to others with stunning frequency. Its predominance as what is, by all indications, a virtual calling card comes about not only as a function of the lure of the screen but also as a consequence of the 180-degree turn that may have been seeded, early on, by a singular moment in American cultural history.

ON CHRISTMAS DAY IN 2006, TIME MAGAZINE PUBLISHED ITS ANNUAL "Person of the Year" issue with no actual person. Instead the cover featured a photo of a computer, on top of which lay a small, reflective paper rectangle— a makeshift mirror floating above a single, captivating word: *You.* Nodding to the then newly minted capacity to customize one's online presence, this comparatively brazen editorial conceit perfectly captured a sense of where things appeared to be heading. American culture stood at that moment on the precipice of a new, self-obsessed democracy: for the people and by the people—and photographed by the people, too. With that seminal issue, we were told to get ready for our close-up, and get ready we did.

We took the bait, eager to recalibrate a kind of carpe diem for this, our brave new world. Over the ensuing years, we dug ourselves in deeper: we posed and we posted, crafting public autobiographies that were perhaps less a function of who we were than what we aspired to be. Digital posture became our new religion. We hovered expectantly from post to post, pumped up on clickable hearsay, self-appointed ambassadors of our own tautological tales. The culture of "you" rapidly shifted—from collaborative filters and customizable metrics into the closed feedback loops of so much social media—and, before long, we were awash in an endlessly self-referential data feed of pokes and likes and tweets. Fast and unforgiving, we kept on keeping on, only to find ourselves, over time, trawling in a counter-Copernican spiral of irrepressibly parochial circuitry.

Time, as it turned out, got it all wrong. It wasn't really ever about "you" at all: it was about *me.*

Today, a mere decade after that seminal Christmas cover, the photographs posted on Instagram (often bearing the stunningly unimaginative tag #me) currently number in the hundreds of thousands. Photographing oneself has become a singular and popular pastime, an instantly rewarding yet indisputably time-sucking activity poised somewhere between narcotic and sport. Welcome to the new narcissism: look at me, like me, comment and retweet and hashtag me. Warhol's "fifteen seconds of fame" have effectively devolved into a serially renewable data plan. This is selfie culture, writ large.

Ah, the selfie. Could there be anything more culturally pervasive—or more achingly masturbatory? And what purpose does it serve, other than to remind us how reflexive we've become, how reflective we've ceased to be? Has the mesmerizing reality of that inward gaze become so seductive that we have lost sight of a bigger picture, a world beyond ourselves? If the self-generated management of one's own profile is tricky, what's trickier still is the degree to which others can pierce the veil seemingly protecting your identity. Identity theft is not uncommon, but privacy theft is worse; leaking personal data can have humiliating, if not lethal, consequences, begging the question: how does what we make represent who we are?

A recent Department of Homeland Security white paper carefully articulated the benefits to 3-D printing, not least of which is the fact that these devices are capable of reproducing human tissue, including—but not limited to—skin, intestinal segments, bladders, and bones. Once ethically questionable, trafficking in human organs may soon become beneficial in health care practice, particularly, we are told, in impoverished countries. (On the flip side, there is nothing to keep do-it-yourselfers from producing, say, weapons.) Perceptually, this kind of innovation does not come without a cost, and as beneficial as it may seem to simulate human life through advances in science, robotics, and the wonders of modern plasticity, there are fundamentally *human* limits to all of this.

"Immersion" entertainment, the great promise of virtual reality headgear, is capable of significantly destabilizing the body's perceived equilibrium, thereby inducing waves of nausea in unsuspecting players. Big and bulky, such headsets are steely cocoons that shut out the world, privileging a staged reality over an actual one. To the extent that your identity is a function of the milieu in which you exist—which is to say, the collective influences of a broader cultural network of people, places, feelings, and ideas—the designed headset reverses it all, placing you in a kind of self-imposed visual lockdown. As a social construct, VR reinforces the selfie's inward gaze in spades.

The "uncanny valley" is a theory in aesthetics suggesting that the close but not identical visual reproduction of human qualities can result, for certain viewers, in feelings of physical revulsion. The more lifelike the features, the greater the chance that certain spectators will experience unpleasant triggers—primary among them being an unbidden, sudden fear of death— which is experienced involuntarily but suddenly and deeply, like whiplash. Lifelike yet robotic, the avatars that populate movies and video games and even our homes are the destabilizing products of a fertile, if ultimately myopic, imagination: they're designed to "resemble" the human form, a caricature of the normative.

Consider, for a moment, the manufactured identity of the bespoke adult mannequin—the sex toy—designed to perform, let us say, on cue. Clad in silicone, powered by Bluetooth, these anatomically idealized dolls can now open their mouths to speak, revealing lips and teeth and soft, fleshy tongues. (In the world of the uncanny valley, where unexpected anxiety about one's own mortality is experienced like a full-on sensory tsunami, this raises the concept of *petite mort* to new and worrisome levels.) Such futuristic design interventions propose that robotic performance can be tweaked and torqued against an imagined spectrum of anticipated human needs. The very idea hinges on an assumption that we humans are somehow inadequate, and that we can choose to amend these inadequacies through certain sly design interventions, a questionable maneuver—machine-managed appearances, porn as progress—clearly no longer merely the domain of science fiction. "It has become appallingly obvious," wrote Einstein nearly a century ago, "that our technology has exceeded our humanity."

Einsteinian prognostications notwithstanding, and given the chicken-and-egg question of design and identity, how far does one go to introduce the self into selfhood? While artificial insemination offers a solution to infertile couples, related interventions can easily slip into designer territory, making design appear shady and reframing identity as a set of curiously "curated" actions. Can design be more than a tool for just managing appearances? Assuming the answer is yes, what are the moral parameters guiding our choices and governing our actions? A same-sex couple chooses a gestational surrogate only if she is willing to have her eggs fertilized by each partner, separately: the couple's "designer twins" are born nine months later, each child perfectly resembling one of the participating fathers. Is this a design intervention, or a scientific one? A gesture of control, or conceit? A calculating act of self-preservation, or a stunning act of hubris? While it is not our role to judge, how can we not at least ponder the conditions framing the questions, conditions that frame a culture to which we all inevitably contribute?

If personal identity displays itself to the public through primarily visual means, it is not such a stretch to imagine a day in the not-so-distant future when we can self-curate to a degree not merely reliant upon the screen. We are, all of us, autodidacts when it comes to technology, and as such we are exposed to—and the beneficiaries of—a remarkably widespread range of options for identifying and distributing ourselves across networks. Some of these methods are visual. Many, too, are viral. And all seem to hinge on the often at-odds twin principles of free speech and implied privacy. Their nexus, often the sweet spot for trouble, is visual: pictures project identities like torpedoes, slicing through the air, across cultures, past the boundaries of the forbidden. One has only to think of the *Charlie Hebdo* attacks in Paris in the early winter of 2014 to understand that identity is iconic, that satire is a sacrilege all its own.

In design parlance, the word "identity" generally refers to a brand: someone else's brand, which, with a designer's guidance, comes to be governed by a recognizable set of coordinates that collectively frame its essence and ensure its individuality. A corporate identity system or program extrapolates this from, say, a basic logo or wordmark to something more far-reaching and powerful: that same logo should work on a business card and on a truck, in print and online. Successfully executed, it becomes the formal fulfillment of a company's philosophy, representing its core values, its very intention and spirit—its public face, if you will.

Such efforts tend to succeed admirably in the face of business practice, but where individuals are concerned, the options are less clear, making a sense of personal dislocation perhaps inevitable. Surely this is the case for any well-known person whose photo has been published without permission, for those who are victims of privacy leaks and system hacks, or for anyone unfortunate enough to experience both of these together. We are all a function of that amorphous, distributed gestalt that has, of late, manifested through our online profiles—all of us capable of being reverse engineered by the very components that delivered us to that public stage in the first place. We can—indeed, should—be mindful of what we show the world, how we show it, perhaps asking ourselves with some systematic regularity why, indeed, we need show it at all. To the degree that we self-publish, we cede control to a larger community of friends, as well as strangers, co-conspirators, even enemies. We will, in all likelihood, each have 3-D printers at the ready in the not-too-distant future, poised on the precipice of that as-yet-unknown future orbit, ready, if nothing else, to print out our own bones. Indeed—we can. But that doesn't mean we should.

Chapter Four: Consequence

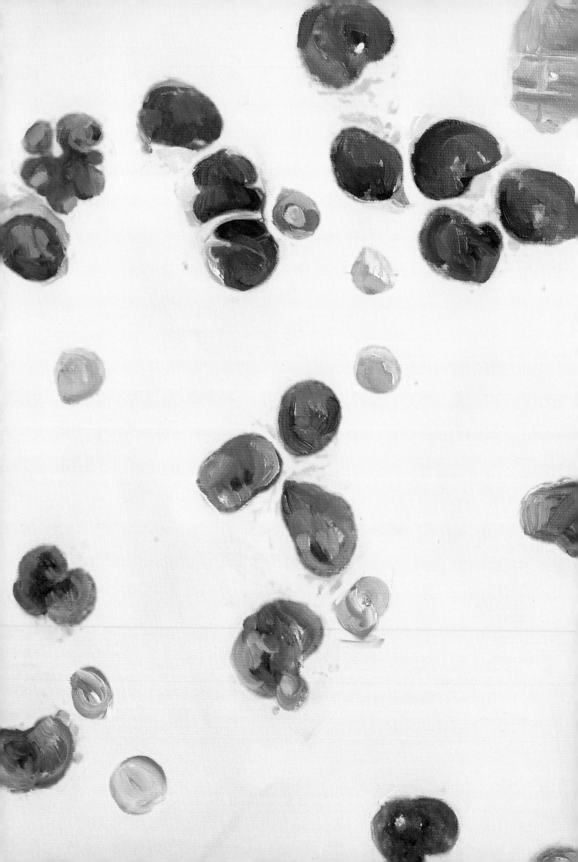

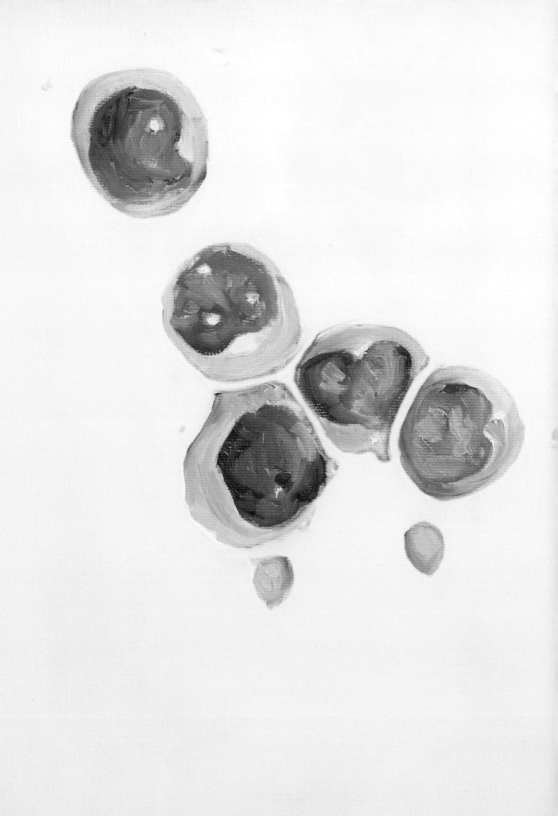

SOME YEARS AGO, A GRADUATE STUDENT OF MINE CREATED A SCREEN saver tied into data feeds about death-row inmates: unlike the scores of benign images to which the idle computer typically defaults, here, at last, was something emotionally gripping, something tethered to real time and real life. Several years laster, another student designed a shoot-'em-up video game in which the "shooter"—upon successfully annihilating his or her opponent—was subsequently obliged to interact with the victim's family: this project, too, sought to link recreation with reflection, connecting physical cause to emotional effect. And only last year, two design students in Geneva collaborated on a powerful project to address the rarely discussed personal issues raised by the visualization of postmortem digital identities.

All of these were student projects—which is to say that they were not, in principle, intended for commercial distribution. (Interestingly, too, all three were designed by women.) Yet each raised questions about design as a dynamic tool and, more important, as a catalyst for human interaction, for deeply considered emotional response. It remains true, if unfortunate, that these sorts of considerations are acknowledged so infrequently, and to the extent that we are each producers as well as consumers, it is also rather alarming. While we allegedly consider the impact on the greater good—being mindful of the environment, for example, and how contributions to the landfill compromise both our individual and collective health—we often fail to question the subtler ways in which the things we create and consume might produce deeply unintended consequences. And indeed, they do.

In physical terms, there are bizarre examples, beginning with the shortsightedness brought on by love. Yes: love. How else to defend the woefully aberrant thinking that led so many well-intentioned couples to place clunky metal locks on the Pont des Arts in Paris, only to compromise the beauty (not to mention the safety) of a perfectly nice bridge? (The keys themselves were tossed into the river, another morally questionable practice.) This bulging bridge of brass—the American critic Adam Gopnik later called it a "rashlike infestation"—became, over time, a kind of symbol for a particularly modern kind of poor judgment (and to others, for misguided tourism), a public visualization of the consequence of so much multiplied selfishness. Yes: selfishness. Because, in a deeply human sense, that is the consequence of not thinking about consequence. End of story.

Except, of course, it is really just the beginning.

IRONICALLY, THESE "LOCKS OF LOVE," AS THEY WERE CALLED— approximately three-quarters of a million of them on that one bridge, weighing approximately forty-five tons—can perhaps be seen as inversely proportionate, in both deed and intention, to the American nonprofit organization by the same name, a social initiative founded more than a decade ago on the proposition that many healthy girls and women will willingly chop off and contribute their own hair for others whose medical conditions have, for a variety of reasons (ranging from alopecia, for instance, to various kinds of cancer) predisposed them to hair loss. At its core, this organization known as Locks of Love seeks to restore feelings of self-confidence to others, an extraordinarily compassionate act that anticipates the needs of someone other than yourself, which is one very basic way of defining consequence in human terms. Another way, perhaps, is to read such interactions on the basis of pure cause and effect. In the case of the American foundation, the motive is altruistic; the method sacrificial; and the result at once meaningful and scalable.

The happy couples in Paris? Not so much. Here the motive was egotistic, while the method was random, sloppy, and imposing. And the result? A clunky, dangerous eyesore. Kant once wrote that it's the motive that matters and not the consequences, and indeed, lovers—giddy optimists that they are—find motivation in their sheer happiness, happiness they feel compelled to share with the rest of the world (or at least the Parisian world). Paradoxically, however, they fear that their love is somehow endangered: therefore, by padlocking their conjoined names onto a piece of Parisian real estate, they're simultaneously reinforcing their own, albeit wishful, immortality. There's a soupçon of schadenfreude here, too: there, but for this lock, go we! (Or, put another way: our good fortune exists at the expense of yours, particularly if our ill-considered decision to contribute to Parisian bridge bulkification jeopardizes your own well-deserved safety. Oops.) True, for many generations people in love have written their names on walls and carved their initials into trees (acts of selfishness, too, especially for the trees), but in this case the idea that one seemingly innocuous act leads to a second, and a third, inflates the physicality of a single gesture to a kind of grotesque visual extreme. Over time, as couples elect to contribute to this folly, the sheer damage caused to public property comes to endanger the collective welfare of a greater population. Oops, indeed.

Perhaps there's an ironic twist in here somewhere: after all, were there not scores of French aristocrats whose hedonism led them, centuries ago, to behave in a manner suggesting that the needs of others did not matter in the least? (*Après moi, le déluge!* Let them eat cake!) Arguably apocryphal— if entertaining—the legacy of devil-may-care elitism endures in France, except that in this instance, the lunacy is reversed: here it is the visitors who reveal their lack of appreciation for anything even beginning to resemble consequence, while, at a civic level, French authorities are deeply concerned. (Paris may be for lovers, but in the end the demands of safety trumped the lure of sentiment: after a highly publicized tug-of-war on this subject, the Parisian government announced that the locks would all be removed, beginning in the spring of 2015.)

Add to this the maddeningly viral growth of everything-sharing, and you begin to wonder whether, at the core of this ill-conceived ritual, there isn't a bigger problem, which is not that one bad decision begets another, but rather the sheer acceleration with which it does so. It's at once staggering and stunningly obvious to think that we've come this far only to share a fundamentally flawed understanding of something as simple as time, but it is precisely this kind of temporal slippage (act now, think later—or think not at all) that's come to underscore so much bad behavior.

To fully grasp the concept of time, of course, is to visualize it: we do so with clocks and calendars, devices that quantify some kind of evidence of demonstrable progress, thus obviating the need to fully comprehend the more uneasy abstraction of time's inevitable passage. To objectify time is to measure it—consider a child's growth chart, for example—which ultimately skews our attention by making everything look like a timed race. We tend, in Western culture, to be almost maniacally preoccupied with the future— expecting our politicians to make policy decisions that will ensure better tomorrows for us all; protecting our children; worrying about our children's children—while we typically view the past (and sometimes the present) as a been-there-done-that waste of time. The typical modern person worries more about download speeds than about soil erosion. We outsource our personal lives, relegating photographs and memory keeping to any number of apps (our phones are smart, so we don't have to be) or to services that preside over what was so we can concentrate on what will be. History can't possibly be doomed to repeat itself, as long as it's all safely stored in the cloud.

Except it isn't safe, and it will repeat itself. Designers are especially complicit in this equation, because we place such a premium on novelty and invention: if history has come to be seen as antithetical to this goal, beckoning to nostalgia is generally viewed as nothing short of anathema. Increasingly, there is substantial evidence to suggest that we view not only the past but the present, too, with a kind of skeptical ennui, powering hectically through all our lived experiences because we know we can log them for review at a later date. (We don't stop to smell the roses: we merely upload pictures of them to Instagram.) Round-the-clock access to nearly everything has resulted in a kind of fun-house overdrive: our capabilities bloated with false power, our capacities displaced and perspectives fragmented, is it any wonder that we've become increasingly impervious to the needs of others? Cue those clunky locks on that exquisite Parisian bridge, seemingly innocent mementos of personal experience gone horribly, inexorably wrong.

If the enormity of brass baubles illustrates the potential for catastrophic consequence at the physical level, the scarcity of forethought in virtual spaces is even more concerning, and here's why. The designed thing online floats about in a state of perpetual dislocation. Thus liberated from contextual constraints, it is subject to sharing, yes; but also to hacking and poaching and meandering down an unseen path that can lead anywhere. Simply put: in virtual spaces there is no irony. And yet, on some fundamental level, irony—like innuendo and nuance and gesture—is one of our most cherished human sanctions, a distinctly person-driven characteristic that is hardly worth sacrificing for the triumph of the quick fix, be it a speedy transaction or a hashtag hootenanny.

Consider the following. A design student at a distinguished university finds a poorly executed piece of video footage, produced by a certain rebel army, complete with bubbly, bright yellow type superimposed over a spooky gathering of men in uniform, guns at the ready. Because the student has been carefully schooled in making form (which is to say, he has a keenly developed eye for observation and, thanks to his devoted faculty, he possesses in equal measure the valuable technical skills that enable him to produce just about anything), he meticulously apes the poor production qualities of the footage—the visual language, if you will, of scare tactics—and essentially retrofits his own message onto the clip. Part design skill, part cunning and subterfuge, the resulting "hacked" video is intended to be posted online, where its cleverness will inevitably be trumped by the far more pernicious reality that the receiving audience will—in the absence of any didactics or staging, without explanation or setup or disclaimer of any kind—believe that it is real.

What's being lost—and what is so critical—is that we acknowledge a profoundly implicit (if largely ignored) Newtonian imperative: the idea that there are destined to be equal and opposite reactions to the things we design and distribute. (There is nothing particularly fun or cool about this: it's just a necessary concept to grasp.) Unintended consequences are far too easy to overlook when inventing something new; it is much more seductive to appeal to a kind of utopian ideal, to convince yourself and those in your immediate orbit that this thing you've made has never been made before, and to get it out there, and fast. More seductive still is the idea that you are somehow channeling a kind of modern-day manifest destiny, besotted by the Internet's endless real estate, where your potential for widespread distribution is limitless. Ironically, though historically used to describe an epidemic to be avoided, the term "viral" has evolved into a deeply desirable commodity, a synonym for public approval and the greatest carrot on a stick of them all— global acceptance. But at what cost?

Now consider this: For a class assignment in a digital media class, students are asked to create an online memorial. How are we remembered and represented after we are no longer here? They are asked to consider epitaphs, obituaries, and all the funerary customs that frame our contemporary understanding of death, and to respond in a screen-based venue. One student, fascinated with the Collyer brothers—whose deaths in 1947 sparked a comparatively early media frenzy—builds a website predicated on the simple notion that it disappears over time. As in the previous example, the form apes the content; but in this instance, the result packs an emotional wallop that is—both visually and emotionally—commensurate with its historically accurate core content. Mirroring the excavation of so many years of saving newspapers and trash, the site is designed to progressively fade away, just as the brothers' lives were, in essence, reduced to nothingness over a period of days, as the police forcibly evacuated all those suffocating piles of stuff.

In a fairly recent episode of the British television series *Black Mirror*, denizens of an anonymous community log hours on stationary bikes, hoping to accumulate enough points to purchase a chance to compete in an *American Idol*-style talent show: the tacit presumption is not only that celebrity is a universal goal but also that there's some direct link between methodical effort and global fame, even if it is achieved mindlessly on a bike. The idea of power expressed as physical exertion—and as currency, or even cultural capital—recalls the scream machines in Pixar's *Monsters, Inc.*, which, while geared to children, nevertheless reflected a wry, caricatured take on crowdsourcing: these were comical, if dystopian, evocations of consequence. (*WALL-E*—another Pixar film—proposed a world where bloated humans would navigate in automated easy chairs, armed with oversized, disposable cups permanently poised for instant beverage refills, lest anyone be obliged to wait for second helpings.) Part comic satire, part science fiction, the what-if scenarios posited by shows like *Black Mirror* and the Pixar films share one thing in common, and that is the degree to which they position the loss of individual will as a consequence of all that is addictively viral, much—if not all—of which is experienced as a visual phenomenon.

The exigencies—and the promises—of free speech stipulate that our capacity to say (and show) what we believe to be worthy is protected by law. To this end and in most instances, the things we make are geared to provoke opinion, which is a primary form of intended consequence. From the advent of the town crier to the development of broadsides, political posters to crowdsourced campaigns, boldly persuasive propaganda to loopy video mashups, designers have always sought to push the boundaries between the self and society; indeed, to track the provenance of design as a subversive activity might lead a devoted researcher as far back as the cave paintings at Lascaux. Arguably, all visual mark making implies the will to say and show something, a tacit desire to formalize a personal viewpoint and the fervent need to share it. But there is some essential component missing from the equation if we deliberately create things that are destined to travel far beyond the purview of our own ambitions, where we cannot possibly anticipate their outcomes, whether good or bad, enlightened or disastrous. Once unmoored from our imaginations, the things we so enthusiastically produce embark on their own tricky odysseys, whereupon they are invariably poised to gain their own momentum, to traffic in their own often unprecedented vulnerabilities. To the extent that students focus on making—and distributing—their work without weighing the broader and more complicated cultural frameworks that characterize civilizations other than their own, we have failed as educators, as mentors, and, for that matter, as empathic individuals, whose job it is to steer the conversation toward something as basic, as critical—and as profoundly human—as consequence.

In the end we must, of course, inevitably go forward but bear in mind the degree to which it can be hard, impossible even, to go back. The physical, social, and cultural repercussions that can emerge from even the most guileless design decisions are likely to be far more indelible than the well-intentioned minds from which they originate. In France, as elsewhere, the "right to be forgotten" currently manifests as a digital initiative, reducing undesirable kinds of social stigma by removing certain incriminating bits of visual evidence online. But that is another kind of consequence, isn't it?

Even and perhaps especially in those interstitial spaces, we are far more likely to remember what we see than to forget it. It is perhaps too easy to assume that given the apparent fluidity with which our communications are being disseminated—fast and furious, trending and viral—the ecosystem supporting them is equally fungible, even forgiving. Fugitive pigments, the blue in certain types of cyanotype printing, for instance, can sometimes recover when light exposure is reduced. The color of litmus paper can be made to change when exposed to certain acids affecting its pH level. But design can never be a willing participant in such controlled experiments. Its impact cannot be so easily harnessed, tethered to predictable, if aspirational, results. Maybe that's the thing about consequence: it can't self-regulate—not without some fallout, some small yet irreversibly potent development, a tenacious and willful fragment spilling out from the sprawling detritus of what seemed, at the time, like a good decision.

Chapter Five: Compassion

IN A REFURBISHED TEXTILE MILL IN THE INDIAN CITY OF AHMEDABAD, four women in saris sit barefoot and cross-legged on the floor. One embroiders in a hoop, while another stitches silently at her side. Across the dimly lit room, two more women kneel above a slice of fabric, gently placing circles of other fabric upon it: gradually a constellation appears, and in her lightly accented—and perfect—English, the only woman in Western dress explains to me what she is doing. "This is Orion," she gestures, showing the emergence of a sequence that begins to resemble a familiar configuration in the night sky. She points to a stack of astronomy books perched nearby. "I'm trying to re-create the stars with the fabric," she tells me, "the remnants, that is."

She is Mona Shah—a textile designer working with Christina Kim of the Los Angeles–based label Dosa—and her commitment to working with recycled material is not only a Dosa conceit but, I soon learn, an Indian one too. This casual collaboration illuminates, perhaps, the degree to which design can function as a kind of international language, and how design operates as a social construct as well.

Founded in 1972 by Ela Bhatt, SEWA, the Self Employed Women's Association (it's also a Hindi word meaning "humble service"), is a trade union that represents 1.3 million women organized into more than eleven thousand producer groups, two hundred cooperatives, and eleven federations in seven states across India, with the greatest concentration of members in the western state of Gujarat. In recent years SEWA has expanded its organization to provide such benefits as savings and credit services, health care, child care, insurance, legal aid, and job training. In 2003 the association created a number of independent nonprofit entities capable of supporting fifteen thousand skilled artisan women from Gujarat. One such enterprise operates three retail stores under the Hansiba brand, so named for an elderly woman—Hansibaben—who was the first rural artisan of SEWA. Her smiling, un-airbrushed likeness graces their branding materials.

SEWA's Trade Facilitation Centre—commonly referred to as the TFC— is a cooperative textile manufacturing company with more than 3,500 artisan shareholders. Rather than a sweatshop of working women, the TFC is employee-owned and produces higher-end—indeed, "design-oriented"— fashion; it has, in addition, begun to produce show samples for many leading designers in Europe and Japan. It also manufactures clothing, jewelry, and textiles for the Hansiba brand, now available not only in India but also for international export.

While approximately sixty percent of SEWA's members lack basic literacy skills, the organization provides sophisticated training on a skills-appropriate basis—so a woman working for, say, SEWA's organic farm (a third nonprofit business cooperative launched not long ago) will acquire math skills as she inventories seedlings, while a seamstress at the TFC, working with patterns, will gain comparable skills related to measuring cloth and understanding pattern making. It is an extraordinary thing to observe: women helping women, providing benefits and engaging one another under a cooperative umbrella of give and take, education and training, growth and opportunity. A member of SEWA's leadership team used the metaphor of a banyan tree to describe this model: "Each member contributes to the strength of the tree's roots," she explained, "while the branches grow independently, sprouting their own blooms."

So it is at the SEWA Trade Facilitation Centre, where hundreds of women cut and sew, measure and mend, bind and stencil. There are neatly queued assembly lines of women, working intently at their sewing machines, braids pulled tightly back as they carry on in an atmosphere that combines quiet diligence with nimble dexterity. The room is silent except for the rhythmic whirring of the overhead ceiling fans. There is no talking. No one wears shoes. Spend one day in the streets of Ahmedabad, with its maniacal motorists and daredevil rickshaws, and you immediately recognize the oasis of quiet that the temple or mosque so brilliantly provides. Step into the TFC, and you realize you've entered a parallel kind of environment. It's a design temple.

It is difficult to describe what constitutes poverty in India, because it's not perceived as poverty so much as a deeply-entrenched reality. There is not a palpable sense of frustration here so much as a spirit of commitment to one's immediate orbit—family, livestock, rickshaw, whatever. People don't stand on street corners and buy lottery tickets hoping for a miraculous reversal of fortune, nor do they aspire to the kind of material acquisition somewhat comically characterized, in the West, by the degree to which we have come to silently genuflect before luxury brands. The entire scale of operation in India is different, partly due to the fact that religion and spirituality play a more prominent role in daily life, but also because there's no time or space—or tolerance—for behaving any differently. In this context, the barometer for what constitutes wealth (money, possessions) is, in a very basic sense, fundamentally irrelevant.

For women in particular, real currency is artisanal currency, so your knowledge of a particular kind of embroidery, for example, simultaneously links you to your family and to your village. It enables a transference of power, in that you pass along your skills to your children as your mother passed them down to you, and within the framework of SEWA's cooperative stewardship, it provides thousands of women with a trade that is at once personally rewarding and, longer term, financially remunerative. (SEWA's business model favors the maker, with 65 percent of the purchase price reverting to the families of the rural women who produce the work.)

The point is to maximize the benefit for everyone: from better use of existing skills, to better access to the people with those skills, to better export of the best of what those skills can ultimately produce. If you consider design as a nonverbal but intensely communicative process, you've got a sense of the degree to which design can function as the connective tissue linking idea to skill to form, marketing to distribution, and back again. Add to this the concept of an outside designer working with local artisans, and you've got an innovative model precisely because it's not a top-down power play: on the contrary, the relationship with the incoming designer—and the process that follows—is managed carefully and respectfully. The big idea here lies in the notion of cross-cultural collaboration, cooperation, and craft.

In this context, SEWA operates not only as a trade facility but more critically, perhaps, as an open atelier for incubating ideas: at present the results are textile- and clothing-related, but there's nothing to say that designers coming here can't be product designers, type designers, or graphic designers. If the point is to use design as an international language, then there's no limit to the potential for exchange and education—which, in all honesty, goes both ways—all of which stems from a compassionate understanding of a world that is bigger than you. At the core of this social apparatus is the idea of compassion for the people whose contributions stand at the pinnacle of the operation. There is a deep clarity about the reciprocity that frames this system, from an exchange of skills and services to a fairness about production conditions and profit sharing. Social yet silent, bounded by respect for families and their legacies, and not a laptop in sight. While it may fail as a model for innovation in the modern sense, it succeeds brilliantly as a forum for personal growth and, along the way, creates a market by and for a constituency that is vital, ongoing, and real.

IMPLICIT IN ANY NATION'S HISTORY ARE TRAGIC STORIES OF THE LOSS
of innocent lives, stories in which misfortune unites us all by reframing what
really matters. Over time we've developed visible patterns of recognition for
such things, public rites that we honor when such events occur. Flags fly at
half-mast. Public lights are dimmed. We bow our heads in silence, but we
do this together, in public, as though compassion must be witnessed in the
company of others in order to be legitimate. People randomly express their
support of historic milestones online by changing their avatars—rainbow-
filtered pictures dominated Facebook the week that gay marriage was
legalized by the Supreme Court, for instance—and there have been reports
of at least one company replacing its colorful corporate logo online with a
monochromatic one in the aftermath of a national tragedy. Does the news
have to be bad for compassion to reveal itself visually? Does brandishing an
icon equal an expression of tolerance? Does it constitute compassion or could
it be possible that we've lost sight of the difference?

The Victorians kept journals of gruesome obituaries to remind them of
their own good luck, a kind personal dossier of schadenfreude—as though
cementing those forlorn tales to the pages of a book provided a shield of
physical evidence that could dispel any similar fate. It was a peculiar display
of compassion—if it can even be called that—but it was a visual response
to the emotions surrounding deep loss, something we rarely acknowledge
in contemporary American culture. On any given day, we read about guns
(which have to be designed) and the deployment of tanks (which have to
be designed), and it doesn't take long before we recognize, almost without
exception, the object lessons that these stories reveal—often with a nod to a
design malfunction. We seldom consider the feats of engineering that enable
piles of metal to soar above our cities, until the tragedies that befall those less
fortunate when they fail to do so. Manufacturers have standards and codes,
benchmarks that protect public safety and are (ideally) recalled when they
don't. Bridges are made to stand, but what happens when they don't?

Loss in general (and death in particular) is the obvious human trigger for what we think of as compassion, if indeed we think of it at all. When we do stop to consider loss, the point of entry is often material: bolstered by the orbit of our stuff, this is death by proxy. We lose wallets, mistakenly jettison papers, and fail to back up the digital evidence of a host of efforts that follow us through life—files, mostly, but also apps and e-mail and pictures. A friend whose phone bit the dust tried in vain to salvage his photographs, many of his only child. When it became clear this was impossible, he was referred by the support team at Apple to their bereavement counselor.

It is only when we identify the deprivations of loss that we pierce the veil of human compassion. Losing your only child's un-backed-up baby pictures is a kind of loss with which we can all identify, not only because of an absence of physical proof but because of our human incapacity to rationalize the power that our possessions continue to retain. Yet it is equally if not more jarring to witness the absence of demonstrative compassion evidenced by gestures that illuminate a lack of understanding, a paucity of feeling—stupid things people say or do, glaring errors in judgment that frequently take the form of a physical gesture. "For years after our mother's death," wrote Thomas Bernhard in a short story entitled simply "Mail," "the Post Office still delivered letters that were addressed to her. The Post Office had taken no notice of her death." It is this simple gesture of observation—literally *taking notice*—that perhaps best identifies the compassionate act, and is, for that matter, widely considered a core competency in design. And if taking notice of others is not, in and of itself, understood as a valuable asset in contemporary culture, then why do it?

We do take notice, but of ourselves, not others, and we are rewarded not so much for compassion as for a kind of self-referential vigilance, for watching out for ourselves. This is borne out with stunning regularity in social media, where we count our followers like currency, building out our personal databases of look-at-me links like the unstable bully pulpits that they are.

Do such gestures of self-aggrandizement constitute true acts of compassion? Hardly. Is it any wonder, then, that the value implicit in this essential human gesture is absent from so much of what we make, so much of what we do, so much of how we are represented in public, online and elsewhere?

In the addiction-prone world of video games, we become, over time, just as inured to the visual stimulus of repeated violence as we are to the media deluge of any public tragedy: worse, to the degree that some of these games take their cues from historical fact, we blur the line between fact and fiction, between a real story and its pumped-up retelling. There is no time to reflect or react: the target is external, a dedicated bull's-eye that summons the gamer's single-minded purpose and indefatigable ambition. Writing of the thorny relationship between gaming and guilt, the *Guardian*'s Keith Stuart notes that this is potentially problematic "for designers hoping to create narrative experiences of true depth and meaning."

The degree of depth of feeling that emanates from compassion may lie at the core of this conflict, at least in the world of video games. If you're not rewarded for compassion, why expect it? If your daily activities do not mandate a deeper sense of connectedness to another person, why seek it? Online game expert Nick Yee titled his excellent 2014 book *The Proteus Paradox* as a nod to the mythical Greek sea god who could alter his appearance at will. This, he posits, embodies one of the essential promises of online games: the ability to reinvent oneself. But it's also a nod to the sleight of hand that comes with visual reinvention—a moral slippage that's seldom, if ever, discussed. Design can be alluring in its chameleon-like tendencies, encouraging us to remake and reinvent and redesign as though such efforts are the basic touchstones of human progress. But this kind of design—the kind that focuses on persistent change and serial reinvention—stems from a kind of single-mindedness that can be spectacularly wasteful. It is also, in a word, compassion-free.

The role of design in video games is particularly powerful because it is so often inseparable from the operational aspects of the game itself. Indeed, a resulting subindustry known as "gamification" deploys aspects of game design and mechanics to encourage a particular audience in changing a behavior, learning new skills, or engaging in innovation. In principle you "win" by playing the game, not by increasing your understanding of your opponent, or by staying true to yourself, or, perhaps more to the point, by behaving honorably.

In the United States, where scores of preteens routinely bear witness to all sorts of horrors by just looking at their local newspapers; where PG-13 film ratings offer Sensurround accounts of all kinds of violence, corruption, and evil; and where the disclaimer "Viewer Discretion Advised" is as likely to precede a cable documentary on the dangers of high-risk teen pregnancy as a news feature on prison conditions in the Florida Panhandle, the United States Holocaust Memorial Museum in Washington, DC, discourages visits from children under the age of twelve. This rationale suggests that crimes against humanity are too hot to handle—ergo, we shouldn't teach the Holocaust to eleven-year-olds by encouraging them to identify with other children, because that's just too close to home.

To see discomfiting evidence is troubling, but to protect our children by pretending it does not exist is far more troubling still. Bearing witness to atrocities can be traumatizing to younger viewers, but to deny their existence, to forbid someone from seeing something historical and true, proposes a questionable, soul-suppressing practice. Serge Klarsfeld, a Jewish lawyer and historian, devoted the majority of his adult life to the study of the French children of the Holocaust. His magnum opus—a book that lists the names, addresses, ages, and deportation details of virtually every French child sent to a concentration camp during the Second World War—should be a mandatory staple in every school library on the planet. It is not necessary to witness the unspeakable horrors that befell these children in order to relate emotionally to their stories: one has simply to look through this book, at those children's faces, to begin to comprehend the degree to which compassion is at least as important a lesson for schoolchildren as memorizing the dates of famous battles. Eleven-year-olds need not be exploited, or traumatized, or overwhelmed by tragedy to understand despair and its profoundly human consequences, but they do need to actually feel something to really remember, and ultimately respond, as citizens of a world that they will one day inherit.

The fact that the point of entry is a visual one, and that someone had to have made design decisions to frame and compose what we see—whether on screen or elsewhere—makes the question of compassion a critical and a crucial one, yet it is rarely included, let alone focused on, in discussions about design. Why? Is it because we assume that the presence of a moral compass is implicit? If so, implicit in whom—the sender or the receiver? The designer or the audience? Should the work itself drive us to consider the deeply human convictions that tell us what is right, wrong, uncomfortable, intolerable, unknowable? Is even reaching for answers to such questions a presumptive conceit—or a human imperative?

WHEN THE WORLD-RENOWNED DESIGN AND CONSULTING FIRM IDEO recently partnered with a palliative care doctor to explore better ways of designing the experience of dying, the initial goal was to open up the conversation, to examine points of entry that might be better articulated as a result of a process of design inquiry. In truth, the preponderance of brightly colored acrylic afghans in grim hospital settings reads, to the visually sophisticated, like a catastrophic assault on the senses, and designers cannot be blamed for wanting to fix that. But the IDEO team wanted to dig deeper, to examine the underlying emotional needs of the broadest demographic imaginable—because, let's face it, none of us are getting out of here alive.

Their research did indeed oblige them to consider the pivotal role of compassionate outreach—which they achieved in the form of an extraordinary collaborator, a young, dedicated palliative care physician whose self-described Zen approach to hospice care made him particularly well-suited to lead from a position of authentic and deeply skilled understanding. But the process itself was stunning in its almost comedic limitations: reports of group-think brainstorming sessions conjured images of genuflecting before aphoristic Post-it notes, and parodied what was, in essence, an unimaginable assumption. Who are we, any of us, to design the end-of-life experience for ourselves, let alone for someone else?

Spokespersons for IDEO claimed they saw death as a "big opportunity," and set out to explore how they might capture this not insubstantial market. The underlying notion—*that designers can change the conversation*—was based upon the assumption that rethinking problems is a creative process, and that rethinking design problems is what designers do best. Fair enough. But at the core of this inference is the idea that death is a design problem: that the designer has any right to do this, or any training to do this; that the designer is, him- or herself, capable of externalizing the multiple factors—personal, spiritual, medical, cultural—that may frame another individual's final days on earth. The team of notably earnest death designers were later asked what they had hoped to accomplish. "Best-case scenario is that more people in more places talk about death in a design-rich way," said Paul Bennett, the team's leader, who framed the project as "just another design challenge." ("I don't want death to be such a downer," he later added.)

The very notion that death could be seen as a design challenge raises serious questions about design and about designers. (And perhaps about death.) Who are we to presume that design could ever make a difference in something so quintessentially grim, so epic and mystifying and permanent? Dying is about being dead. (And you keep on being dead, forever.) The inherent lunacy of the IDEO venture is perhaps self-evident. Yet efforts to "design a better death" are widespread: from experience designers in Sweden rethinking the "future of death" by inaugurating a competition to design a new, commemorative set of rituals; to a humanitarian architect in Rotterdam examining the physical properties and formal taxonomies of mortuaries; to jewelry designers who blend human "cremains" with gemstones so you can wear your loved one as a sparkly bauble; to product designers who combine them with additional materials—from plastic to potassium nitrate—to make pencils, fireworks, even dildos; to textile designers creating biodegradable, seeded burial shrouds so your loved one can be "reborn" as a garden; and finally, to scores of graduate theses investigating the visual totems that circumnavigate mourning, bereavement, and the seemingly illogical supposition that you can actually interrupt the stages of grieving with some kind of design intervention. In 2009 two PhD students at the University of Toronto coined the term "Thanatosensitivity" (from the Greek Thanatos, the daemon personification of death) to refer to design that seeks to integrate the facts of mortality, dying, and death into traditional user-centered design.

Invariably, such initiatives quickly reveal the subjective limits of our capacities, illuminating the degree to which we are destined to design for ourselves—for our own personal needs, our own closely held memories, our own metabolic, idiosyncratic, DNA-specific, and ultimately inevitable encounters with the finality known as death. That we have come to process this myopic bubble as compassion is a deeply misguided notion, strengthened, in all likelihood, by the self-limiting tautological loops of contemporary technology. We are, all of us, empowered to do so much: why not manage death, too? Future generations will, with any luck, view as a joke or cautionary tale the fact that a group of well-intentioned adults once devoted significant money, time, and effort to rebranding death.

In the interim, spend any extended amount of time in a hospice facility, replete with its gentle, if preternaturally quiet, stillness, with smells and sounds that linger in your heart long after you've left the building, with the sheer incomprehensibility of loss and the powerlessness of human suffering and the inescapability of all those damned neon afghans, and you realize that design has no true actionable role to play here. Interventions that are aesthetic might soothe the eye, even trick the soul, but they are panaceas of the most benign sort. Understanding that, and accepting the limitations of what design *can't* do, might be—indeed, will very likely be—your greatest act of compassion yet.

Several years ago, Columbia University announced a new program in narrative medicine, defined as "an emerging clinical discipline that fortifies the practice of doctors, nurses, social workers, therapists, and other caregivers with the knowledge of how to interpret and respond to their patients' stories." Their website stresses the importance of something they term "narrative competence" ("the ability to recognize, absorb, metabolize, interpret, and be moved by the stories of illness"), which—aside from conjuring images of residents in white lab coats sitting around reading Susan Sontag—sounds plausible. (Who but a group of doctors would use the word "metabolize" to explain storytelling? Brilliant!) Ninety miles farther north, at the Yale School of Medicine, first-year doctors log time at the British Art Center looking at Constables and Turners: the goal is to park their diagnostic skills at the door and use pure visual observation as a way into seeing something—or someone—else. By formalizing the act of looking in this way, new pathways of understanding are opened, and observation itself is reframed as a compellingly reliable methodology.

That both of these programs use creative methods to elevate clinicians' understanding puts compassion front and center, not simply as a diagnostic tool but as a deeply humanitarian conceit. Ironically, positioned against the multiple staccato interruptions of so much external noise, the inception of these sorts of efforts—literature partnering with science, art partnering with medicine, humanity tethered to reality—shifts the classic model of storytelling to new and considerably more compelling degrees of interest by reminding us that, at the end of the day, real stories are all about people— people who live, and who will eventually die. Grasping that reality is not a design challenge, but a human one.

Chapter Six: Patience

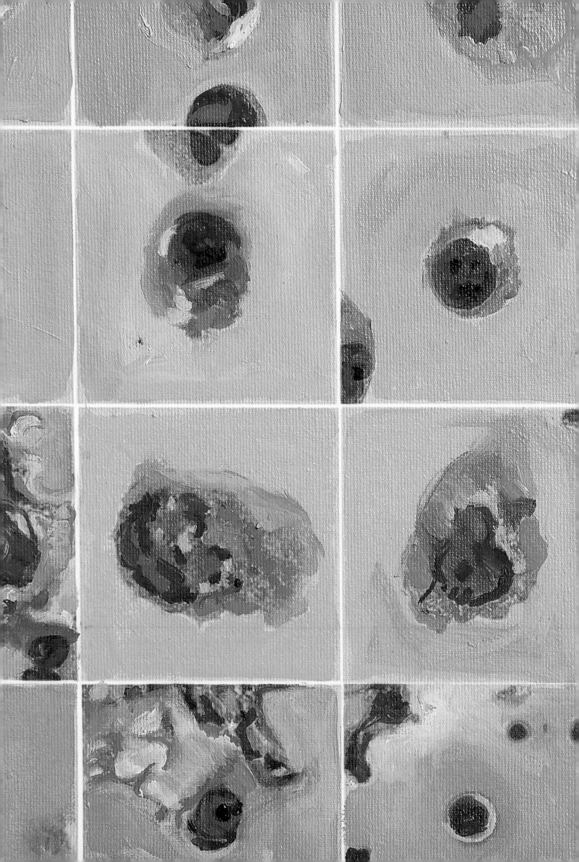

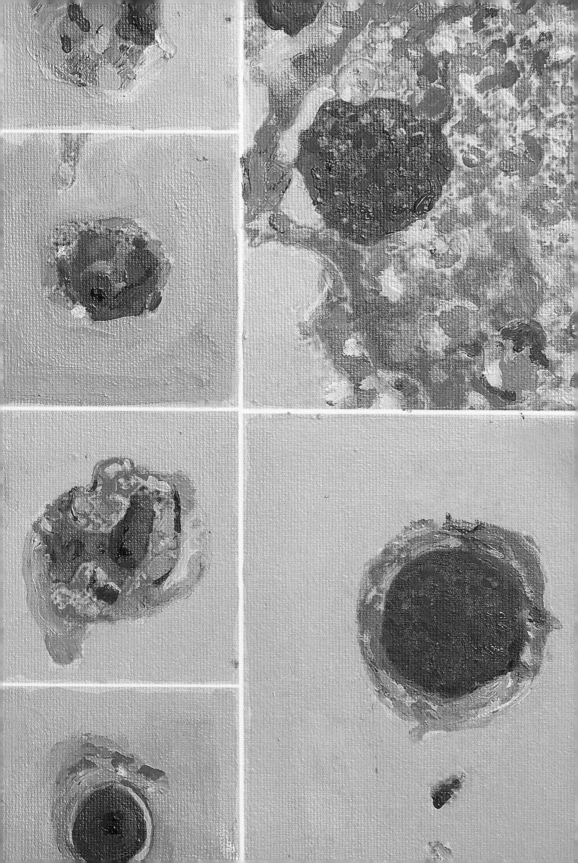

IN HEINRICH HOFFMANN'S CLASSIC ANTHOLOGY, *DER STRUWWELPETER* (*Shock-headed Peter*), there's an endearing fable about a little boy who cannot pay attention to anything. Like all of the stories in this nineteenth-century collection, "Johnny Look-in-the-Air" is delivered as a cautionary tale: he is scolded for "looking at the sky and the clouds that floated by," which make him "often easily distracted by extraneous stimuli." Rhyming couplets aside, the story itself offered a comparatively early nod toward a social predisposition that has increasingly become the rule rather than the exception. Today distraction is a phenomenon with which we are all too familiar—at once a cultural affliction and a behavioral hiccup, albeit one that doesn't seem to go away. But what does it actually look like?

Empirically speaking, there's rather a clear artistic precedent for all of this—at least in Western culture. If the late nineteenth century was framed by the polite rituals of Victorian decorum, the early days of the twentieth century veered brazenly in the opposite direction. Gone was the evocative mystique of fin-de-siècle romance, and with it the static photograph, the reverential portrait, the general air of formal deference that had characterized so much in the manner of classical production. In its place came a whirlwind of ideas and a multiplicity of forces—ideological, mathematical, technological—and all of them unequivocally visual. If nineteenth-century symbolism pushed gently against accepted notions of all that was literal, the Cubists (followed quickly by the Futurists) attacked the entire fourth dimension, fracturing picture planes and with it, our entire psychological grasp of pictorial representation. From language to theater, from painting to photography to film, the first twenty years of this new century witnessed a radical period of exhilarating and transformative change.

At the very center of this change lay the way we considered actual pictures themselves. Using varying perspectives, multiple exposures, and bold sequences of images, Étienne-Jules Marey and Eadweard Muybridge had, by the turn of the century, begun experimenting in earnest with new ways of thinking about kineticism. Soon, moving pictures would enter the cultural mainstream: silent, black and white, and barely a minute in length, combining image and movement in one intoxicatingly dynamic medium. By 1915 D. W. Griffith would move the camera itself, shifting both our visual and emotional readings of visual storytelling—coincidentally, the same year Einstein's theories of the space-time continuum would be made public.

By the First World War, newly modern evocations of streamlined form would reveal themselves as the harbingers of an unprecedented set of visual coordinates. The word "modern" would become synonymous with all that was shiny and new, but it also came to be seen as a synonym for all that was unadorned and efficient and fast. Shorter hemlines made it easier to walk quickly. Speedier locomotives made it more efficient to travel quickly. Soon we had faster cars and planes to get us where we needed to go; and, within the century, an entire assortment of portable technologies promising, if not always delivering, uninterrupted connectivity along the way. If distraction would eventually come to be acknowledged as the inevitable consequence of the twentieth century's love affair with speed, patience has been this century's greatest casualty.

In France, the verb *patienter* means "to wait," while a *jeu de patience* is a puzzle. In Britain, patience is a card game, played solo (Americans call it solitaire). There is a Gilbert and Sullivan comic opera titled *Patience*—a satire on the aesthetic movement of the 1870s—and, as a name for girls, it was unusually popular among Puritans in the years following the Reformation. The infirm awaiting medical help are also called patients, as if to suggest they must possess this virtue in spades to persevere during all those egregiously protracted waiting times. Indeed, the very word "patience" originally implied a kind of suffering or forbearance, implying the time it would take to do something. Implied too was the idea of fortitude and endurance, a nod to an implicit kind of stamina, personal strength, and capacity to self-regulate. At the core of this essential human practice, quite simply, lay the act of waiting.

Recently I went to look at an apartment to rent in Paris. It was dark and cramped, far from public transportation, and ultimately unsuitable for my family's needs, but what struck me the most was that although it had several bedrooms, there was only one toilet. I thanked the realtor for his time, but not before remarking, apologetically, that in the United States, we were simply accustomed to a closer bedroom-to-bathroom ratio.

"Oh, madame," sighed the weary realtor, as though this was not news to him at all. "In France we know how to wait."

The idea of reinforcing a nation's cultural superiority via the pretense of bladder control seemed at once comical and ludicrous, until I realized that he had a point. Endangered though it may be in these computationally dominated times, in certain parts of Europe—Spain, Italy, Portugal, and France, for example—patience remains a deeply valued cultural practice. These are, after all, the sorts of places where the hot lunch is highly ritualized, with multiple courses served with proper flatware, and where coffee is experienced from a porcelain as opposed to a paper cup. This is the territory of fresh markets, long lunches, and postprandial naps. There is a stunning visual preoccupation with food in Mediterranean culture, from how it is sourced to how it is harvested, prepared, bought and sold, served, and, naturally, how it is consumed. At a Paris outdoor market late last fall, I watched a half-dozen people each waiting their turn as the woman being served explained to the butcher in what can only be described as Talmudic detail exactly why she needed two very thin slices of roast beef for her lunch the following day. Her soliloquy went on for a good five minutes. No one would have dreamed of interrupting her.

Conversely, there are numerous branches of Starbucks, in the United States in particular, where professional mobile headset-wearing handlers are on hand to swiftly relay orders from the queue to the barista, lest you be obliged to wait for your piping hot cardboard cup of bespoke coffee. (Preordering via their app is a more common way to condense the waiting period, which, frankly, isn't very long.) Purchasing tickets, ordering dinner, online dating, airport check-in—all these activities are now performed effortlessly not in line but *online,* obviating the need to queue up ever again.

For the Irish writer Samuel Beckett, waiting was at once a psychological abyss and a theatrical trope. For the American artist George Tooker, it was a closed, grim loop of purgatory. What is it we wait for—time's inevitable passage, and our own incapacity to derail it? To exhibit patience is, therefore, to accept the fated reality of this inescapable limbo. Far easier to do the opposite, to barrel on through and stay busy, even if the activity is all too often transparent and meaningless. In his landmark book *Faster,* the American writer James Gleick reflects on the woes of modern-day acceleration, observing, for example, that when confronted with the numbers on a microwave, a time-pressed person is more likely to press "33" than "30." (He includes himself in this demographic, and I confess I'm right there with him.) In a parallel example, visitors to the Louvre are believed to spend, on average, only about fifteen seconds in front of the *Mona Lisa.* Typical time spent reading a newspaper online? Approximately a minute, which sounds like a lot until you compare it to the twenty-seven minutes those same readers formerly spent perusing the printed version. Even St. Peter's Church in New York has begun rethinking modern pastoral outreach with regard to digital economies of scale: now eager to lure younger congregants on Easter Sunday, they've begun experimenting with live-tweeting the Passion of Christ in 140-word increments. Brevity may be next to godliness, but is it wrong—sacrilegious, even—to abbreviate the Bible into Twitter-compliant sound bytes? Or is it just realistic?

Media scholars like Gleick (who writes about a larger syndrome of insatiability and boredom) and Sherry Turkle (who examines patterns in computational behavior and social dislocation) have rightly observed that technology enables us to juggle multiple activities at the same time—or to file and save them for later, neither of which suggest that we place any value on patience at all. And why would we? Ours is the age of the express elevator, the six-second video loop, the listicle. Expressing his own, albeit comic, frustration with the culture of impatience, the comedian Louis C. K. brilliantly skewers smartphone users, capturing the exalted expectations of the connectivity-addicted. "Could you give it a second? It's going to space!" he rants. "Or is the speed of light too slow for you?"

Increasingly, we can't economize enough on our own schedules, choosing instead to exercise a kind of personal power by proxy: we save time by buying other people's time. Human-powered apps like Uber and Shyp let us outsource errands, presumably so that we have more time for ourselves—and to do what, exactly? Current mobile consumption statistics suggest that Americans are spending an average of five hours a day online: after social media and e-mail, by far the most popular leisure activity involves video. (This tells us two things: one, that pictures continue to speak louder than words, and two, that pictures that move are more desirable than pictures that don't.) Nevertheless, most people still resent having to wait for the time it takes a given video to load. There's even a name for this: the Wadsworth constant is an Internet axiom alleging that the first thirty percent of any video will likely be skipped because it is assumed that it contains no worthwhile information. Indeed, when it comes to visualizing something onscreen, the average human attention span is considered to be in the six-second range. Asked how they determined this to be the ideal duration for a video short, the founders of Vine—which has become a new benchmark for addled attention spans—reported that they believed five seconds was too little, but found seven seconds to be an eternity. An alarming statistic, particularly considering that the average goldfish can concentrate for nearly nine seconds.

Can patience be crafted, imposed, designed? In the notable tradition of the French artist Sophie Calle, whose work examines intimacy and trust (and involves following and taking her cues from anonymous people), the artist and filmmaker Miranda July recently introduced an app called Somebody that dispatches strangers to deliver and "perform" messages, literally slowing down and humanizing the "social" in social media. In a similarly human vein—here gesturing to the bygone days when actual film required both chemistry and patience to render an image—there's an app called One-Hour Photo that requires waiting a full sixty minutes before seeing the pictures you've just taken. (Another app, Authenpic, only permits twenty-four photos at a time and requires waiting a full week before they arrive, printed, in your physical mailbox.) Elsewhere, intentionally flawed color is used to bestow a false history on contemporary picture taking, rendering everything "older" and, by conjecture, more seemingly "authentic." Certain retro camera apps—from the faux muted tones of the Hipstamatic to the audible click-whiz of the fake Polaroid—have relegated the whole idea of patience to something so analog it has become the stuff of nostalgia. This, in turn, begs the question: if impatience is indeed a cultural reality, do we consume things differently as a result? Do we design them differently, interpret them differently, remember and record them differently? Do we, in fact, remember them at all?

Oddly, in certain instances, the goal may be to remember nothing: not to retain, but to jettison the very thing you've just created. Users of the currently popular app Snapchat, for instance, engage in a casual practice (and a vaguely cynical one) where images are intended to be eminently forgettable. The premise is simple: pictures self-destruct only seconds after they are sent, which means that you can't possibly be held accountable for whatever it is you've just done. (On the other hand, you also have nothing to show for it.) If the "right to be forgotten" stands at one end of the sentiment spectrum, Snapchat is its evil twin: this is planned obsolescence, writ small. This may at least partly explain its popularity among millennials, a demographic group often targeted as the top-tiered sinners in the war on patience: hyperconnected, perpetually distracted, they are beholden to technologies that both reinforce and reward their unwillingness—if not their sheer psychological incapacity— to slow down. In a series of recent studies by the Pew Research Center, it was speculated that upon reaching adulthood in the 2020s, this generation will stand a significantly increased chance of harboring cognitive impairments: a severe prediction, but one not without some merit. Put another way: if impatience is reinforced by instant gratification in general (and by so many reward-giving visual boosters, in particular), how will this generation be prepared to meet the expectations of, say, real life?

Consider this simple conundrum: When a death is announced on Facebook, the go-to reaction is to hit the "like" button. The visual and emotional limitations of this practice are staggering, not only because our technological sophistication sits so far from our communicative capacity to express complex emotions, but also because we lack the visual vocabulary to do so. And what does the thumbs-up emoticon actually communicate? I like that you shared this? *I feel your pain?* The Victorian custom of sending black-framed condolence notes through the post may seem ridiculous to the time-pressed denizens of social media communities, but let us remember that this classic ritual was once held in check by a rather brilliant design conceit. Instantly readable—the black borders connoting death—the black-edged condolence note immediately telegraphed the purpose and poignancy of the information it contained. Upon receiving such a note, you might just experience any of the following feelings: Sympathy. Empathy. Loss. Grief.

You "liked" none of them.

How is it that we have progressed this far without a common visual vocabulary commensurate not only with our yearning for efficiency but with the arc of our emotional lives? Millennials, of course, are not alone here. Emoticons—those goofy hieroglyphic symbols that proliferate in the texting universe—have become a kind of emotional Esperanto for us all. Where time is concerned, we willingly relegate words to symbols, inadvertently sacrificing the nuance of language, the human prerogatives born of feeling—in sum, the expression of emotion as a personal and interpersonal privilege—all because patience, in the modern world, sits so far down on the priority list.

We are, in fact, constantly searching—not in a personal, self-questioning sense, but externally—each time we click the search button. To the extent that online experience is dominated by the truncated language of the keyword search, and given that search engines drive the lion's share of activity online, then what controls the "bounce rate" (Internet parlance for the amount of time any of us will spend on a given site)? Psychologists often refer to something called "confirmation bias"—in other words, that once we've seen something we like, we'll work hard to insist that it is good, even if it isn't. ("I can never un-see that" is a new refrain, common in social media commentary of late, that might be said to effectively summarize this behavior.) First impressions being what they are, the impact of the visual— a great deal of which, it bears saying, is highly subjective—plays a huge role in what we think as we carry on. Simply put, many if not most people actually do judge books by their covers. Snap judgments are thus born, and while they may happen in a split second, the tenacity of their impact can— indeed, will—linger on.

A snap judgment is, after all, the territory of the elevator pitch (originally a Hollywood conceit, this is a short summary of an idea that should last no longer than the time required to ride an elevator a few floors), which has evolved into a kind of reductive code for creative brilliance: put another way, your idea is only a good idea if it can be explained fast. Fair enough. But seen through the lens of the snap judgment, there is also something called a "halo effect," a term coined nearly a century ago by the distinguished American psychologist Edward Thorndike, who suggested that, for example, an attractive person is believed to be more trustworthy than an unattractive person. Ergo, something well-designed is going to be deemed instantly desirable and will, as a result, inevitably be met with success.

This becomes problematic when you consider, for instance, that a well-designed website is expected to lure (and, even more important, retain) visitors for more time—in essence, ensuring a better (slower) bounce rate—even if its essential purpose is pointless or its functionality is flawed. The very idea that staying power is defined by leaving power is strange: even the term "bounce rate" sounds like a game. The notion of measuring a value proposition against its capacity to entertain ultimately makes everything a game, one that rewards impatience, minimizes complexity, and infantilizes us all.

AN ARTIST I KNOW ONCE TOOK HIS STUDENTS OUT TO THE WOODS, where he had them stand in a cicle. He asked them to walk slowly from the periphery to the center of the circle, and to do so over the course of a minute. He then instructed them to return to their original spots, only this time to take an hour to do so. The idea was to physicalize the experience of time in a radically different way: unhooked from media, they had to construct their own metrics, reflecting upon their own capacities to determine personal frameworks for measuring time, to redefine for themselves what it means to experience the passage of seconds into minutes into a single hour. The reactions were mixed. One student gave up and sat on a tree branch. Another sat down and began a detailed examination of insects on the forest floor. In the end, without the constant interruptions that have come to frame our daily odysseys, this assignment in enforced slowness led to new ways of seeing—which, in the absence of the beeps and the bells, the clocks and the computers, was extremely difficult. (Yet, for some, highly instructive and deeply gratifying.) Can minimized distraction result, for any of us, in renewed patience? And can the things we thus begin to create, even crave, become more thoughtful, more considered, more relevant—even more human as a result?

Perhaps the real question is this: will we come to regret our impatience with patience? Will we look back and wonder why we moved so quickly that our lives were recorded only in passing, our diaries comprising a series of banal status updates, hollow and shallow and long past their sell-by dates? Will we regret our reliance on push-button mapping, on split-second transmissions, on souped-up speed? Will we bemoan relegating paper to the trash heap, dismissing it as old-school technology, ignoring its value and intricacy and depth? And along the way, what kind of story will we leave behind, through our morphed and manipulated paper trail—provided, of course, there is any trail at all?

In the end, patience, as John Ruskin once observed, is nobler than beauty, probably because it is so much more difficult to achieve. It takes 250 milliseconds to blink but a lifetime to understand what you see; no matter how much you yearn to speed things up—connection speeds, bank transactions, the postal service, your adolescence—does it really matter? In an age in which patience is a dying art, so too is the time it takes to consider, form, and deliver an opinion, an activity that favors the reflective moment over the reflexive one. Patience, like the moral introspection that inevitably accompanies it, should not date nor should it require its own app to remind us of why it matters. We benefit as a species from so many things, but being in a hurry is not one of them.

Chapter Seven: Solitude

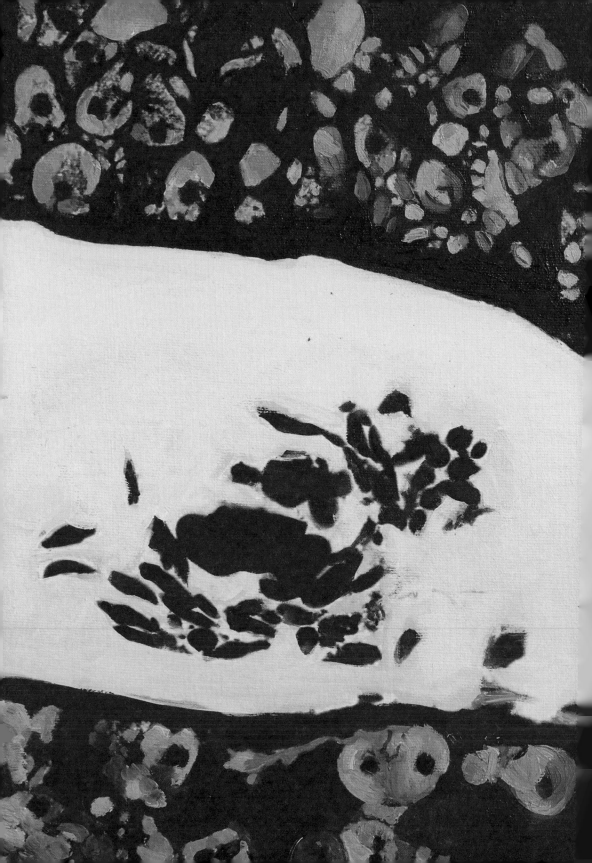

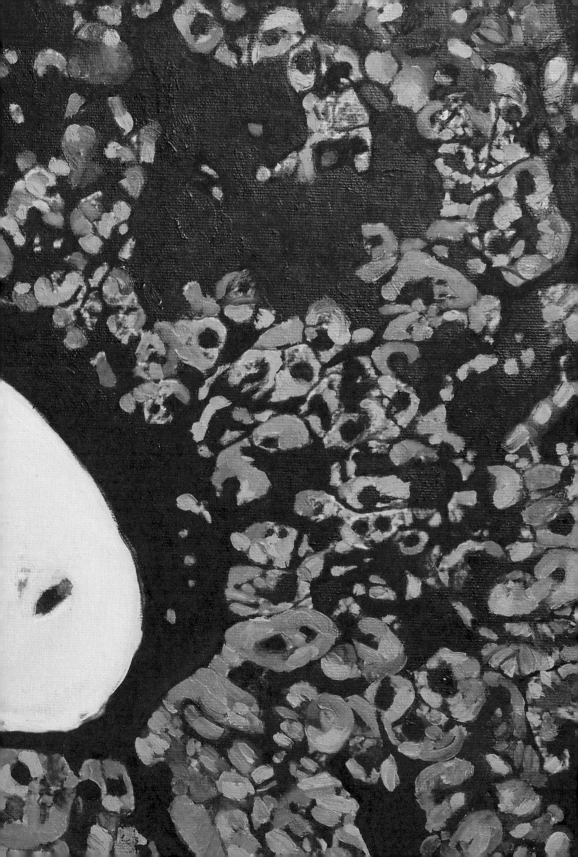

AT A MACWORLD CONFERENCE IN 2007, HEWLETT-PACKARD'S THEN design chief Sam Lucente took the notion of co-creation—the idea that the client is an active rather than passive participant in the making of something new—and restaged it as a value proposition for designers. As a corporate designer, Lucente had a point. There was a pragmatism and a transparency to this approach that seemed novel, even daring, coming after so many years of market testing and focus groups, behaviors that benefited strategists but essentially polarized the creative process into a hierarchical playing field, a binary system dividing makers from receivers. This idea of hands-on collaboration between designer and client was seen by many as a crucible, particularly by those involved in certain dynamic industries where the platforms and possibilities were changing at a dizzying pace: software developers, media companies, tech startups, and social entrepreneurs, among others. But by positioning design as a primarily service-driven task, Lucente also effectively torpedoed the critical importance of designing things alone, casting doubts upon a process that favored, in his words, a questionable reliance upon "brilliance and magic."

Lucente was not alone in this view: indeed, far from it. Over the course of the last decade, numerous books have championed the value of co-creation, with entire conferences and curricula springing up in support of prototyping in teams, producing things in groups, even touting the creative value of crowdsourcing as an exceptionally democratic kind of professional practice. There's something refreshingly honest about this kind of teamwork: it carries with it an implicit checks-and-balances system, a personification of diversified risk. It's social. It happens in real time. It assumes that if a lot of people make a thing together, maybe there's a better chance for that thing to actually succeed.

On the other hand, who actually designed the thing?

This is not so much a question of ego as a function of economics: as such, let's not for a moment denigrate the power of magic but rather reconsider its pivotal—and profoundly human—role within the creative process, particularly with regard to the innovation cycle. And that begins, quite simply, by spending time alone.

Solitude has long been heralded by poets and artists, scientists, and even politicians as a catalyst to original thinking, albeit a paradoxical one. What Kafka called "a cold abyss" and Rilke dubbed "vast, heavy, difficult to bear" was to Wordsworth the definition of sheer bliss. At once a factor of isolation and an offshoot of recreation (the flaneur, after all, walks alone), it seeds independent thinking and bolsters bravery. ("Without solitude," writes the literary critic William Deresiewicz, "the solitude of Adams and Jefferson and Hamilton and Madison and Thomas Paine—there would be no America.") As a profoundly human condition, solitude is at once difficult to achieve and near impossible to sustain, perhaps because there is no way to tell whether we are doing it correctly. (The late American film director Mike Nichols once said the same thing about directing, which he likened to sex: you never watch anyone else doing it, he wondered, so how do you know whether you're doing it right?) "Here, in my solitude," wrote an aging Ingmar Bergman in his diary, "I have the feeling that I contain too much humanity."

Yet there remains something ineffable about solitude, something pure and honest, because it obliges us to face truth, to dig deep, ultimately to reach something hard-won and, by conjecture, to create something new. How is it, then, that we have come to value the group creation over the individual one, the conversation over the monologue? How can something be deemed original if its success is ultimately measured by consensus? How can the power of design—indeed, the visionary power of anything—be privileged when it comes from a team, rather than an individual?

When did co-creation become the rule, rather than the exception?

Such thinking stems from a business model rather than a creative one, which may, at least in part, help explain where the derailment all began. As a concept, co-creation grew out of an article from 2000, initially published in the *Harvard Business Review*, in which the authors described it as what it was: a business strategy. That this notion surfaced at the dawn of the sharing economy made it irresistible to anyone seeking to build a product, grow a business, yield a market share—but it did so at a cost. In spite of the degree to which portable technologies have made it increasingly possible to work alone, co-creation advocates lobbied for the opposite. In this new century, innovation was soon acknowledged as a collective rather than solitary pursuit. And so, it seemed, was design.

On the other side of the cultural spectrum, those same portable technologies that freed us from our desks also paved the way for a new artisanal culture of iconoclasts, with new initiatives (including global entities like Etsy and regionally scalable ones like Maker Faire, among others) protecting precisely the work-in-isolation model seemingly endangered by the co-creationists. In this new environment, do-it-yourself making soon became a popular cultural model. From recycled materials to rekindled methods, solitude has come to be recognized by many as a desirable yet ultimately temporary condition, to be accessed and subsequently retired from active duty the moment you choose to connect. And because social media allows you to connect effortlessly, and from a distance, that time spent alone becomes somewhat precarious, even phony.

And just what is it we're sharing? Fleeting glimpses, memes and tropes, regurgitated content produced by others? In many cases, we don't share; we *reshare*, positioning ourselves not so much as makers but as carriers, aligning ourselves as the purveyors of so much trivia, supporters of the eminently forgettable, participants in a spontaneous assembly line, a delivery mechanism of any number of random things—for what is more terrifying than being alone, staring at a blank screen or empty page, peering head-on into a creative void? Far easier to redesign and retrofit, to appropriate and go from there.

And here's where it gets tricky: if we're not favoriting and forwarding anonymously, we're claiming some modicum of ownership, merely by association—which at its core is stunningly inauthentic. The world of collecting was once driven by the economics of auction prices, but now anyone with a Pinterest or Instagram account can claim to basically "own" every Paul Klee drawing ever made, merely by gathering digital reproductions and uploading them to share on a designated bulletin board. First Amendment rights protect certain essential freedoms, one of which appears to be that we can take pictures of pictures, reposting and reinterpreting them, molding and modifying them, retrofitting them into our own self-generated narratives. Such acts of random sharing are disconnected from the thing itself, raising questions of authorship, ownership, and citizenship, because once we can no longer protect what we make, does our responsibility to that thing likewise subside? Perhaps if we spent less time consensus building in groups and more time asking hard questions on our own, we'd know the answer.

Yet if co-creating is problematic because it homogenizes the singular vision, so too is the social isolation of this new cultural climate, one framed by so much perpetual, if artificial, connectedness. Plugged in but tuned out, we don't always make decisions that are appropriate. Is it because we make them alone? Because we make them too quickly? Strategically, this may inform the degree to which the groupthink approach in design invokes more methodical requirements that fall within the purview of something called "best practices"—an attempt to rationalize those same requirements, to make them adhere to some kind of professionally ratified playbook. In the effort to honor "best practices" (and who says they're the best?), the very practice of design has fallen prey to a more pragmatic, if constrained, set of definitions: method supplants magic, teams trump individuals, and design—visual and accessible, the most democratic of art forms—becomes our new, if marginally devalued, common currency.

To be fair, co-creation is not now, nor has it ever been, the same as collaboration, which operates from a decidedly experimental position, unconstrained by anticipated results or qualified, for that matter, by projectable outcomes. At a moment in history when social governance restricted political and artistic expression, members of the Dada and Situationist movements actively experimented with the idea of resisting certain kinds of order by making things together. Within this comparatively novel practice was something called an "exquisite corpse," a kind of relay race of art making in which the verses of a text or the rendering of a drawing were produced in successive installments by different people, each producing work at different times. From Dada to Situationism, from Futurism to Fluxus, such collaborative experiments expanded to involve time and space, sound and movement, and what would come to be seen as comparatively radical new approaches to materiality, language, and performance. The participants in 1960s "happenings" reveled in such explorations, some of which were media-agnostic while others were spontaneously random, chance-driven, and dazzlingly media-complementary. The artist Robert Rauschenberg did not "co-create" with John Cage and Merce Cunningham, but they did collaborate, because they made things, each of them independently, one at a time—each of them, in that moment of truly making something, acting alone.

Collaborations succeed best when they are more than the sum of their individual parts, recontextualizing what we see and, in so doing, obliging us to reconsider our expectations through chance or serendipity. Such subtle shifts in perception recall certain Dada artists whose work brilliantly invoked the principles of defamiliarization, a term coined in 1917 by the Russian theorist Viktor Shklovsky that operated on the simple premise of presenting common images in unfamiliar ways—collage, for example. During the early years of the Weimar Republic, collage in general (and photocollage in particular) was used to question order and dislocate perception, indeed to question reality as it had been previously portrayed. The politically charged collages of such artists as Hannah Höch and Raoul Hausmann derive much of their power from a kind of visual appropriation that combined artistic deviation with social dissent. So jarring was this work when it initially appeared that when first exhibiting their own collages, certain artists (John Heartfield among them) took to showing the work alongside the newspapers from which the materials had been plucked, on the assumption that viewers would otherwise fail to fully grasp their original context. Such pictorial mashups were unsettling (so unsettling was Hannah Höch's work that she was later called a "degenerate" by the Nazi government), which was precisely why they were so extraordinarily powerful. By availing themselves of existing phenomena—advertisements and magazines, newspapers, and photographs—the resulting work drew upon existing conditions, opinions, and cultural propositions, reclaiming the visual language of a highly politicized, public vernacular. What quickly emerged was a kind of graphic satire born of courage: formal dislocation as visual slippage, appropriation as anarchy—all of it a function of acute observation and individual voice. That's not hacking. That's originality.

To be truly original demands time spent alone, just looking, and looking hard. Quoting David Joselit, who sees fine art as a series of deep reservoirs containing temporal experience (he calls paintings "time batteries"), the art historian Jennifer Roberts instructs her Harvard students to spend multiple hours alone looking at a single image. To Roberts the gulf between looking and seeing requires, by sheer force of pursuit, a ruthless solo engagement. She is keenly aware of the external pressures to conform to a host of social and technological dynamics that pry students away from this kind of visual concentration, and her pedagogy reflects this. Perhaps because their work, by its very nature, demands a focused kind of solitude, fine artists understand this practice implicitly. A painter I know recently remarked that for every hour he spends painting, he spends two to three hours just looking. Designers need not consider this an indulgence but rather a critical feature in thinking and making work, a recipe, perhaps, for a more engaged kind of invention. Concentration demands bravery, and that is best achieved by acting alone.

For visual makers in particular, observation manifests as a distinctive kind of concentration that both sees something for what it is and tries to imagine what else it might become. For the late, experimental American filmmaker Stan Brakhage, this resulted in extraordinary explorations of many things—including, among other things, the life cycle of a moth, caught on adhesive strips of tape and subsequently captured on film, where it regained, however briefly, the magnificent illusion of mobility. In the 1960s Brakhage lived a quiet life in rural Colorado, where he made films and his wife Jane kept scrapbooks that combined writing, drawing, collage, and poetry, literally availing herself of the detritus on the cutting-room floor. Constrained by a scarcity of funds as well as materials, she sketched with found objects: the scrapbook, in this sense, became a kind of movable canvas for testing ideas that weren't quite two-dimensional but weren't time-based, either. He looked close. She looked wide. Their work in either case benefited from deep connections to what was right there in front of their eyes.

Working with wide strips of cellophane packing tape, Brakhage captured fleeting things—among them, blades of grass, pieces of flower petals, dust, dirt, and the diaphanous, decapitated wings from insects. His process revolved around using the tape to produce a series of facsimile filmstrips: wider than the elegant Super 8 mm that was his hallmark medium (the resulting work, *Mothlight,* a mere three minutes in length, was shot on 16 mm) but long and geometric, they're a suite of attenuated rectangular portraits. The idea of using adhesive tape as a photographic medium (which is effectively what it is, capturing something in time on a single surface) represents the simplicity—indeed, the sheer brilliance—of one man's indefatigable effort to visualize a single idea. In this work Brakhage created a world of disembodied shapes where life is rendered as silent and inert, only to be revived into these hauntingly beautiful abstract patterns. One becomes suddenly struck by the realizations that these compositions preceded his idea for them (they led, and he followed) and that the intensity of this formal exercise would not have been possible in a room full of people making decisions—or indeed, making anything—driven by the imposed dynamics of the group.

Solitude, as it happens, presumes a certain core competency in reflection, something that requires not only space but time. (Brakhage may have been poor, but he had both.) It's a slow, often thankless process of trial and error, generation and iteration—but at its core, it is really about seeing—near and far, inside and out, understanding the personal, the individual, the self in the selfie. For time-pressed designers, faced by budgets and clients and deadlines, physical isolation might seem an untenable working paradigm. But is it? In contemporary culture the act of working alone is often cast as counterproductive, while the opposite is equally (if not more) likely to be true.

Design is, at its core, a social discipline. But that doesn't mean its gestational growth does not, to a considerable degree, benefit from the ruthless objectivity that comes from imagining alone. In the end, while design practice may remain largely characterized as a collective endeavor, the core design idea—that lightbulb "aha" moment—still originates in one person's mind. As such, it gives birth to that which is truly original, what Thomas Mann called "beauty unfamiliar and perilous," as unpopular and as disconcerting— and as lonely—as that might be. Solitude, in this context, is tricky: it's not so much the creative incubation chamber as the rudderless foundation.

Locating that anchor takes real time, time spent alone, and nobody ever said that was easy. ("There are days when solitude is a poison that makes you beat your head against the wall," observed Colette.) If you feel you need to colonize a crowded coffee shop to be creative, think again: this is pretend solitude, with earbuds. Because to really be alone is to hear the world, and what you hear is not always what you want to hear. Or, for that matter, what you want to see.

Chapter Eight: Melancholy

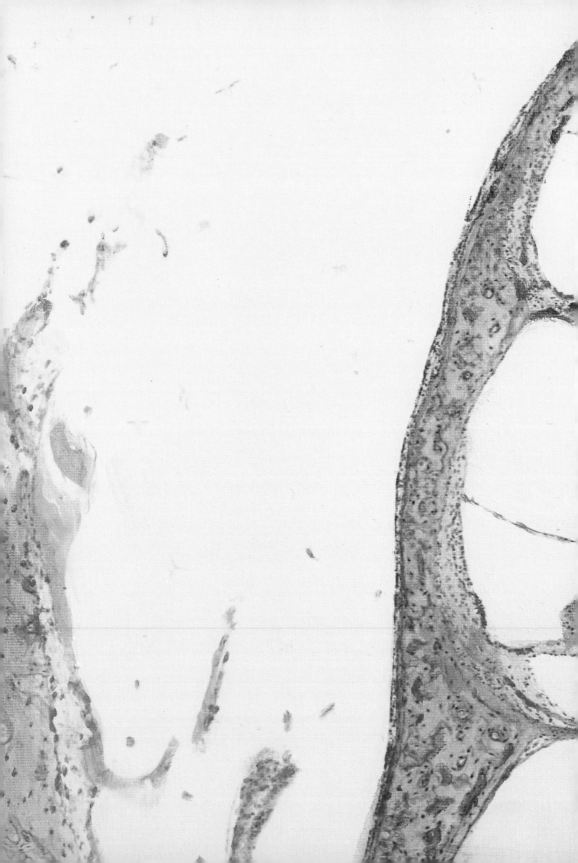

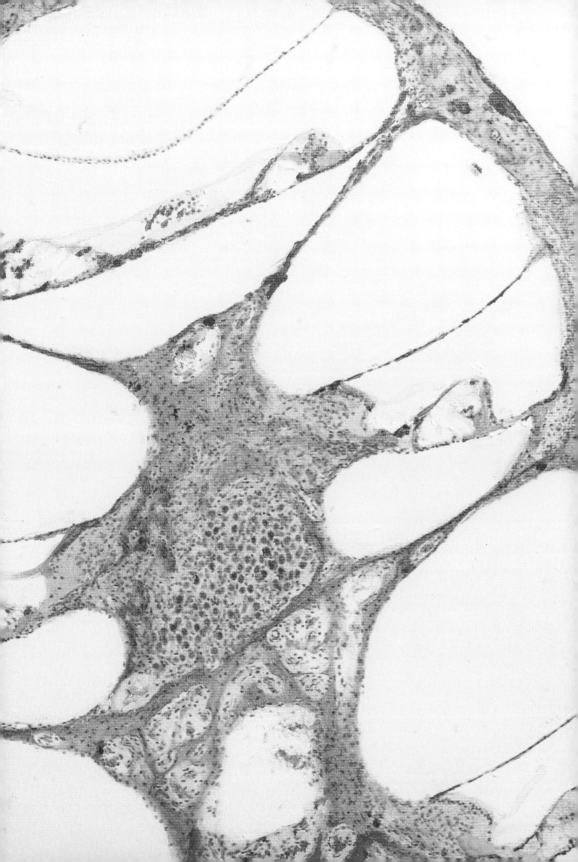

I GREW UP SURROUNDED BY PICTURES OF DRAMA AND TERROR AND death. My father collected public health posters, and our house was filled with oversized, captivating broadsides in which fear and frolic were provocatively conjoined through pictures and words. *Syphilis! Tuberculosis! Scarlet fever!* That they were propaganda was meaningless to me; after all, I was a child, with no independence or power of my own, so exercising any suggested behavior prompted by a poster's message was out of the question. (Though surely the implied cautionary tale—*become sexually promiscuous, and you will contract syphilis and die*—could not have been lost on my well-intentioned parents.) Still, these huge confabs of typography and layered image were the visual hallmarks of my immediate orbit, literally flanking my passage from the reliable safety of home to the untold mysteries of the outside world, and providing what I would later come to see was my introduction to graphic design.

Many years later, as a graduate student at Yale in the late 1980s, I was exposed to the parameters of what design could be, and here my struggle to reconcile form with emotion was hopelessly stalled. While I begrudgingly acknowledged the importance of my formal education, the prevailing aesthetic orthodoxy was anathema to me. How could you produce design for human beings and deliberately drain it of all human content?

I have spent a good part of my adult life trying to answer precisely this question.

At the time, the prevailing wisdom maintained that the true power of design lay in chiseling it down to its purest form: it was only when it was unencumbered by sentiment that design could truly deliver on its modernist promise. To inject personal voice was to deviate from this no-nonsense objective, and one was best advised to resist such selfish, subjective impulses. Better to hone your craft and minimize your imprint, remove yourself from the work and focus on the most salient, most germane form your message could and must take. The designer's mission was straightforward: to create the simplest, most harmonious, most neutral form, thereby enabling communication to the widest possible audience.

Oddly, none of us dared challenge this hypothesis, because it was widely assumed that our design ancestors had struggled nobly against years of oppression to drag themselves out of the murky propaganda brought about by war and commerce and, God help us, commercial art. We were the lucky survivors. It bears saying that most, if not all, of my professors had come of age in Europe during that postwar period at the dawn of the International Style, a time in which the profession privileged clarity above all else. As the chosen disciples of this noble tradition (adherents of the Bauhaus, the Basel Kunstgewerbeschule, and Black Mountain College, whose principled faculty and alumni had bravely brought graphic design to America), they dutifully subscribed to a don't-rock-the-boat view of design education—indeed, of design itself. Their general perspective was one that privileged formal rigor over personal voice, seeking the most reductive solutions to life's most complex problems. Such were the visual manifestations of Cold War reserve, the seeds of which had been sewn and its resultant pedagogy firmly established in the canon.

This never sat well with me. It occurred to me then, as it does now, that life's most complex problems are the same: war is war, death is death, the world evolves, but the basic problems do not essentially change. That styles come and go is a given (Victor Moscoso's 1960s civil rights protest posters were as visually representative of the generation in which they were published as the one I'm about to describe from 1915), but how is it that sometime between the Eisenhower administration and the Summer of Love, an entire generation of designers virtually abdicated responsibility where the true representation of human experience was concerned? And that we were encouraged to do so in the name of design?

Consider the following: a poster, published in 1915 by the Boston Committee on Public Safety, following the sinking of the *Lusitania*. The image was based on a widely circulated news account from Ireland about the tragedy, which claimed the lives of more than one hundred Americans. "On the Cunard Wharf lies a mother with a three-month-old child clasped tightly in her arms," wrote one journalist. "Her face wears a half smile. Her baby's head rests against her breast. No one has tried to separate them." No one tried to separate them, indeed; nor did the artist, Fred Spear, attempt to separate image from sentiment, news from art, form from content. It remains even now a chilling and unforgettable picture—a mother and her child swept into sudden death, which, in conjunction with a single word—"Enlist"—creates a message of ferociously simple impact.

Some years ago I asked my students if graphic design had ever made them cry. Particularly with regard to graphic design that lived online—where the cacophony of competing messages makes a single, immersive experience highly unlikely. Was such a thing even remotely possible? I asked.

And why, they countered, was this a goal?

The goal, I explained, was to join the manufactured thing—graphic design as an external representation of something else—to the world of the living. The goal was to connect, to enlighten, to more deeply understand. And how can you act if you can't remember? You remember when you feel something, like I felt terror as a small child in a world of oversized public health posters. In a parallel memory, I can also clearly recall feeling terrified by the spontaneous apparition of a station identification symbol in the form of the CBS eye—William Golden's brilliantly minimalist logo—a glimpse of which sent me hiding under my parents' bed. (I was tiny. It was huge. You do the math.) Still, those posters pulled focus; as much as I was haunted by them, I was also mesmerized by their beauty, their theatricality—and that feeling has never left me. Who among us does not hope to create work with such indelible grit, such enduring humanity?

This all bears repeating now, at a time in which so many designers are engaged in addressing design for the public good—design that is sustainable, meaningful, socially relevant—because how can you achieve any of this if you don't engage at some fundamentally human level, a level where memory and feeling are as valued as form and execution? True, nostalgia is still, as it has always been, a bad thing in design. At its best, it's redundant. (At its worst, it's kitsch.) But the opposite is equally vexing, because design that caters to designers, or design that privileges novelty over reality, or design that ignores its basic constituents—design for social change is, after all, design that must be socially relevant, and that means design for and about real people—is just as problematic as design that canonizes modernist ideals in the name of neutrality. Design that strives for neutrality, that seeks to extinguish its relationship to the human condition, risks removing itself from the very nucleus of its purpose, which is, yes, to inform and educate—but also to enchant. To do that means that sometimes what you feel is not the exhilaration of the present but the indelible sadness of the past. And sadness has to be designed too.

PREDATING CERTAIN WELL-KNOWN CEMETERIES IN EUROPE AND THE United Kingdom, the Cimitero Acattolico in Rome is believed to have the largest concentration of well-known graves in the world, which sounds suspiciously like a typically hyperbolic Italian claim—endearing but, in all likelihood, debatable. It sits across from the Pyramid of Cestius (dated between 18 and 12 BC) and is known for being the final resting ground of both Percy Bysshe Shelley and John Keats, the latter having come to Rome in the winter of 1820 hoping to recover from tuberculosis, only to succumb to the disease months later. Keats is buried next to his good friend Joseph Severn, a painter who looked after him during his final illness, and who was apparently so poor at the time of his own death that a posse of close friends paid for his interment—an impressive crowd that included, among others, the Italian poet Gabriele Rossetti. (They're all duly acknowledged in a movie credit-worthy crawl on the back of his tombstone.) Wedged between these stones lies a marker that could only belong to a child, which turns out to be for Severn's son, who died tragically and accidentally in his crib as an infant.

Such woeful narratives are common in cemeteries, and the Acattolico is no exception. If Rome has rightfully earned its name as the Eternal City, it is perhaps at least in part due to the soulful stories on the sides of stone plinths such as these—tales expressing the infinity of grief, the interminability of mourning, a gloom so profound it can only be reflected in a series of gray tablets, protruding from the earth with a kind of deep, solemn grace.

The famous are buried here, as well as the not-so-famous, and what they mostly share is the fact that they were, for the most part, foreign-born. None were Catholic (hence the cemetery's name)—there were Jews, Protestants, and others—and no crosses were allowed on tombstones before about 1870. The gravestones themselves range from early neoclassical to full-tilt baroque, with no shortage of simple, minimalist, even neofascist markers, appearing as barely more than geometric motifs in this otherwise densely plotted park. (There are even plots for pets.) Some include typos—as in the case of the grave shared by two deceased children of the American sculptor William Story—which may have been the consequence of an Italian stonemason's flawed command of written English, although it seemed perfectly logical to me. After the loss of two children, how could anyone possibly be expected to remember how to spell the word "February"?

"It might make one in love with death, to think that one should be buried in so sweet a place," wrote Shelley, shortly before his own final days. His first son, William, who died at the age of three (probably of cholera) is buried here with the poet's ashes. When it came time to bury his beloved wife, Story spelled everything correctly and placed a magnificent weeping angel on her grave. Breathtaking in its immense scale, it can be seen from nearly every position of an otherwise monochromatic site—a smoothly polished white-winged creature, bent over in a sweep of eternal grief.

Like Fred Spear's poster, the elaborate funerary sculpture or sepulcher is a form of visual theater. These artifacts are not trying to sell something, nor are they novel in their expressions of public purpose. But they are no less designed than the newest iPhone, and they may be even more fundamental to our understanding of interpersonal conduct, each a representation of the unthinkable, the unknowable that awaits us all. Both the paper poster and the stone plinth represent actual people, and both require the unimaginable task of collapsing the enormity of human complexity down to byte-worthy scale. Obituaries do the same. (So do résumés.) Cemeteries like these reveal stories that remind us of our own mortality—how could they not?—just as they gesture poetically to a time when war and disease claimed young American and European mothers and soldiers, grieving parents, even innocent children in their tiny cribs. Perhaps, in the end, such imagery reminds us that much as we may crave making and consuming design, first we're people: people who pay taxes and raise children and read newspapers and vote. People who eat and sleep and argue and question. People who laugh. People who remember. People who even, occasionally, cry.

Chapter Nine: **Humility**

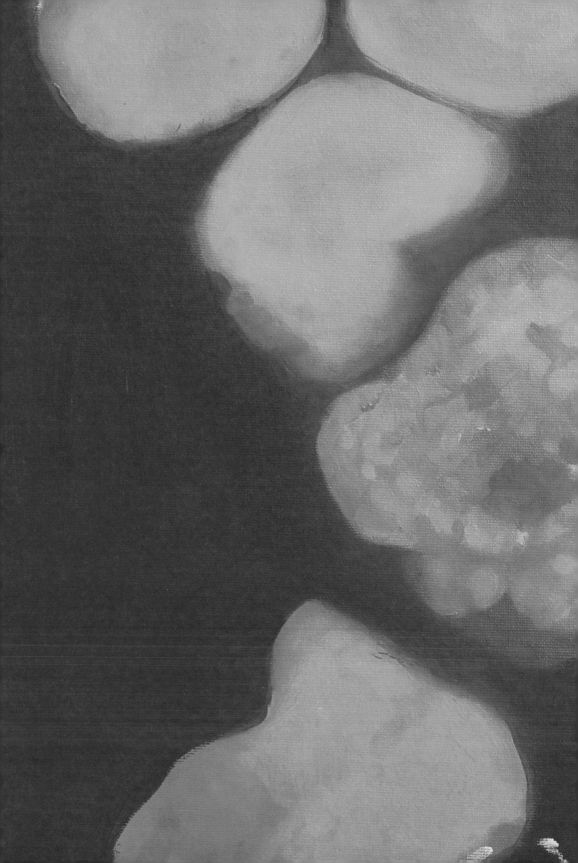

SUMMER 2012. MY HUSBAND FAINTS IN THE GARDEN. THERE IS AN emergency visit to the hospital, where he is quickly examined, transferred to a gurney, and given one of those thin robes that strips everyone of their dignity. Almost immediately he is hooked up to a series of mysterious machines. Minutes trail into hours. Bags of fluid come and go. Shifts of nurses change. Tests are administered—CT scans, EEGs—and blood drawn on what seems to be an hourly basis. There is one endless night in the emergency room waiting for a bed, and then over the course of the next week there will be many beds and many rooms, streams of doctors and nurses, multiple teams of medical students, and many, many more questions than answers. What month are we in, they ask? What is twelve minus eight? My clever husband is given simple memory prompts and fails them all. With each successive test and its results, a new specialist enters the room, each new face becoming a visual manifestation of gathering doom. If it was good news, it seems to me, there wouldn't be any reason for new faces. If it was good news, we wouldn't still be here in the hospital, waiting, endlessly, for answers.

In this clinical setting, my husband is a patient. In the less hygienically protected though no less carefully monitored world outside, people are users. In the virtual world, users are viewers, and viewers are eyeballs. Thus rationalized by such real, if dispassionate, metrics, the average person is swiftly reduced to a digital kit of parts, an involuntary puppet awaiting sentient reconstruction. There are now entire industries devoted to "human-centered" approaches to design (suggesting that there may, at one time, have been a design predisposition *against* humans), approaches that can and do address everything from the way we sit at a desk to the way we walk through an airport to the way we read a newspaper, hold a toothbrush, or eat a sandwich. Yet as humbling as these gestures may appear to the uninitiated, there's no shortage of exaggeration, too, with regard to design's equally lofty claims. From a hospital in Florida that boasts a "birth design team" for expectant parents, to efforts in Sweden where end-of-life care is reimagined as "designing death," the danger is that design, as a discipline, may have begun to veer irrevocably beyond its already pluralistic reach. Is it a verb, a noun? A language, a practice, a faith? Is it a community to be shared, a commodity to be traded? If design now belongs to everyone, can there still be rules—for conduct, for ethics, for those humans around whom we're supposedly centering things?

In a court of law, the phrase "asked and answered" constitutes a viable objection, one intended to derail unnecessary rhetoric. Fair enough; but to assume you know the answer to someone else's dilemma is to miss the point entirely. It is also an expression of unbridled arrogance, perhaps as good an explanation as we've got for the *opposite* of humility. To the degree that blanket access to WIFI makes even the most reluctant autodidact a laissez-faire know-it-all, why ask questions at all? Nobody says "I don't know" anymore, because Google has all the answers, and access to Google, or Bing, or Siri, or Jeeves, or the new Amazon Alexa—a voice-activated electronic box meant to require even less effort in the pursuit of the endless amounts of daily knowledge that fuel our lives—renders curiosity a nonissue. To "not" know is therefore likely to be seen as ignorance, or worse, weakness. Rather than digging deeper, we put the focus back on ourselves, a gesture of self-aggrandizement that further cements the questionable illusion of power and increasingly distances us from honesty, from reality, from humility.

Along the way, designers are reborn as "information architects," strategic brainstorming is rebranded as "design thinking," and anyone tasked with coming up with a creative solution is dubbed a "storyteller." Design plays a role at once reassuring and insidious, because it privileges the package and the performance, rendering a kind of instant polish to almost anything. (This is the territory of false authority.) Once things "look" finished, we accept them as real: instant logos, templated websites, the casual sketch seen as an immediate solution. All too soon, the facility with which visual legitimacy is so swiftly achievable makes it seem as easy to produce an elegant teacup as a convincing terrorist video.

This is what happens when design is embraced by all: it becomes a kind of panacea. We applaud ourselves and each other, trading humility for hubris. And we embrace design thinking as a boon to business, a differentiator in the marketplace. There is a growing body of research suggesting that thinking like a designer provides a kind of exalted cultural currency for a number of reasons, not least because it presupposes a distinct creative advantage. (Indeed: who doesn't want to think of oneself as a creative thinker?) "Recent years have shown a growing preoccupation with the circumstances surrounding the creative act and a search for the ingredients that promote creativity," the legendary American designer Charles Eames once observed. "This preoccupation in itself suggests that we are in a special kind of trouble— and indeed we are."

The process of thinking like a designer, once a fundamental pedagogical given in the atelier, is now something you can study in business school. (In the fall of 2015 the *Harvard Business Review* devoted a full issue to the systemic benefits of design thinking for executives.) Today the very concept of innovation now lays claim to design strategies, prototyping practices, and a host of tool kits focused on introducing this notion of so-called human factors into corporate practice. Aspiring change agents thus consider everything from ergonomics to economics, psychology to philosophy to countless practical considerations, all in the name of design. ("Innovate as a last resort," Eames wisely advised.) Just as ambiguous in its definition, and perhaps equally vexing, is the preponderance of DIY, the do-it-yourself movement, which applauds agency but also presumes a set of skills that remain somewhat nebulous. It's all very nice when you're dealing with selections from the buffet table of material culture—IKEA furniture, for example, or Build-a-Bear Workshops—commercial outlets where preselected menus of options make even the most creatively challenged persons feel like they're eligible for the Turner Prize. But there is another, more insidious subculture at work here, one that is predicated on the notion of *undoing* the work of others, and where the line between sharing and stealing becomes markedly unstable. While creative destruction occurs when something new kills something older (television kills radio, the iPad trumps the newspaper), the notion of disruptive innovation more slyly insinuates itself into the design process by operating as a kind of benign barnacle, the bottom feeders ousting the top feeders by taking root and colonizing subtly but swiftly. If this is a function of intelligent design—survival of the fittest being what it is—then it may be high time that designers begin to question what truly defines their work. This, it would seem, begins with being ruthlessly objective about what it is we actually contribute, which begins with admitting what we know and—perhaps more critically—what we don't.

THE CONCEPT OF DISRUPTIVE INNOVATION FIRST APPEARED IN A 1995 article, coauthored by Joseph Bower and Clayton Christensen and published in the *Harvard Business Review*, that challenged the evolutionary trajectories of more classic innovation cycles. It sounded radical, and it was: the idea was that a product or service would take root at the bottom of a market and subsequently migrate upward to displace existing, established competitors. Fair enough—if you're an economist. But for designers, whose educations do not, in principle, embrace an understanding of market economics, it's not clear that this kind of approach has led to great promise, beyond the degree to which an entire generation of designers have sought to position themselves as progressive simply by adopting this language. In this humility-poor environment, the idea of disruption appeals as a kind of subversive provocation: much like the denizens of Silicon Valley have been said to favor the expression "let's break shit" as shorthand for their own disruptive practices, too many designers think they are innovating when they are merely breaking and entering.

Regrettably, too, many people have come to regard design as a form of hacking, the word itself increasingly used as a synonym for design, and why? To begin with, the term itself has a checkered past. In slang it means someone who's not very good at his or her job. In politics it's a manipulator. (In prison slang it's a derogatory acronym for a guard: literally, it stands for a "horse's ass carrying keys.") In many cities, including London and Philadelphia, a hack is a taxi driver (the word itself is a reference to the era of the Hackney carriage), while in programmer subculture, it is a term that has its roots in the Artificial Intelligence Laboratory at MIT (the mothership of all things computational) where over time it has come to possess an almost Socratic quality. (You "hacked" as a way to trouble-shoot your way through knowledge, just as a theoretician might engage in debate, or a designer in critique.) Nevertheless, its fundamental meaning remains a violent one: to "cut with rough or heavy blows"; to "kick wildly." It's a gash, a laceration—a gesture of attack. That such vituperative language plays a key role in an industry that prides itself on human-centered values is itself questionable; beyond that, it remains troubling in a more philosophical sense, not only because it lacks a certain basic humility but also because it's just jarringly inauthentic. To the degree that design is about invention (which is a synonym for originality, an admirable goal for anyone), perhaps the real question, then, is this: are you still the designer if you hacked someone else's work?

Playful as it may purport to be, the intentionality that begets the effort to hack carries with it a kind of implicit social contempt: to hack is to perceive value only in that which *you* contribute, fundamentally eviscerating the person or process that preceded your intervention. In this view—and it is not insignificant—the idea of hacking comes from a position of arrogance. Whether that arrogance is sheltered by the loose promises of the sharing economy remains uncertain. True, open-source materials are, by their very nature, meant to be retrofitted, built upon, and extended by others; we live in a moment that applauds the so-called open source and privileges transparency, which implies not only that our work is shared but also that we share equally in good intentions, in united goals. (Politically correct though this may seem, it remains, arguably, an assumption with little basis in fact.) Hacking—that maverick-like, invigorating catalyst of disruptive energy—appeals precisely because it overturns expectations, operating like a centrifuge, wreaking havoc, and yes, breaking shit. To innovate via hacking is a fascinating creative construct, but at some point somebody is going to call it for what it is. And that is stealing.

On the upside, the degree to which design thinking has entered the cultural mainstream bodes well for businesses and for the designers who support them; for nongovernmental organizations (NGOs) that work with design practitioners to reinvigorate problem-solving practices; and for a growing number of cogent and increasingly multidisciplinary educational programs that have successfully introduced design within the context of social innovation at the college and graduate levels. This is an upside for us all, and bravo for them—for their insight and perspective and goodwill, and for reminding us that real design is about real people. All of which is indeed good, if not exactly novel. From industrial designer Henry Dreyfuss, whose 1955 book *Designing for People* introduced the idea of the designer as a skilled polymath (thus prefiguring Howard Gardner's theory of multiple intelligences by nearly thirty years); to the modern polymath Ellen Lupton, whose 2014 book *Beautiful Users: Designing for People* takes a contemporary look at usability, maker culture, and the democracy of open access; to graphic designer Scott Stowell's recent *Design for People: Stories about How (and Why) We All Can Work Together to Make Things Better* (part monograph, part crowdsourced compendium, a visual celebration of what might best be described as open-source narratives), design has now successfully emerged from its inward-facing bubble.

Except that a big part of that bubble remains intact. And here's why. Everyone likes things that look good, feel good, and act—well, good. This explains "design for the common good," which, like "designing for people," is not so much tautological as it is mythological. Design, after all, was social media before social media, because it hinged on the very essence of that which, by its very nature, ricochets between the personal and the public: messaging and communication, pictures and words, signage, language, visual reciprocations between the self and society. To imply the opposite— to suggest, in fact, that there is an opposite (designing *against* people?) is as much a misnomer as "human-centered," as inverted a paradigm as, say, design for social good (which implies that there's design for social bad). While we've come a long way from, say, the questionable practices of postwar industrialists who saw planned obsolescence as both a credible design practice and a plausible economic strategy, we can't just keep feeling good because we recycle, or because we print with soy-based inks, or because we only listen to music we pay for. Empathy is not the same as sympathy, which is not the same as compassion. To be clear: you feel empathy when you've found yourself in a similar situation, and sympathy when you haven't. (Compassion, a word that should derive from the word "compass" but does not—it is actually a form of pity—floats around as a kind of understudy.) We think of these responses as though they're "purely emotional virtues," writes the

American essayist Rebecca Solnit. "But they're also and maybe first of all imaginative ones." At its core, humility is artistry.

TWO YEARS AFTER BOWER AND CHRISTENSEN PUBLISHED THEIR ESSAY on disruptive innovation, another *Harvard Business Review* article appeared—this one based upon the idea of what its coauthors, Dorothy Leonard and Jeffrey F. Rayport, dubbed "empathic design." At the root of their then comparatively radical claim was a reconsideration of the simple act of observation: not the clinical, disenfranchised kind of observation that takes place in labs and libraries, but the hands-on, touchy-feely kind that emerges when you're right there in the moment. (Today such focused looking might fall under the rubric of mindfulness.) Here, they proposed, information gathering would take place in the immediate vicinity of the person—in HBR parlance, the "customer"—rather than remotely, thus leading to solutions of greater relevance and, presumably, generating more successful outcomes. To observe a product's real, in situ performance was, the authors posited, a potential boon to all kinds of growth. (They also cautioned about observation in "cyberspace"—this being 1997—and asserted that none of this was intended to replace actual market research.)

There was something refreshingly modest in looking to "empathy" as a design conceit, even if it reads today as a kind of anachronistic throwback to the us-versus-them didacticism of twentieth-century advertising culture. ("The consumer is not a moron," David Ogilvy famously wrote. "She's your wife.") Yet at the time of its initial publication in those late days of the pre-networked 1990s, this article was nothing short of revolutionary, calling out the inevitable biases of what were at the time a set of deeply entrenched rituals in business development. Fair enough; but where does that put us today—and who is to say whether design has a role to play in the context of building empathy, role play being the operative concept?

Describing the slapstick scene created for the lozenge-shaped Bob (modeled after Charlie Chaplin's famous scene in the satirical 1940 film, *The Great Dictator*), *Minions* director Kyle Balda observes that "the biggest goal for animators is to create a sense of empathy." Here is design in the service of despotism, its comedic success a function of the emotional honesty of its creators, reminding us that empathy can be funny too.

A recent report from the UK Design Council proposes implementing design capabilities to "shrink the empathy deficit," suggesting that in order to do so successfully, designers would be well-advised to equip themselves with more classically academic disciplines, including neuroscience, behavioral psychology, and economics—a noble ambition, the results of which, of course, remain to be seen. Empirically, design has long been understood to contribute to a kind of "empathic" engagement because it supposedly put people front and center. Over time such predispositions grew into a recognized approach with regard to design and problem solving, but also quietly contributed to the increasingly myopic allure—and closed feedback loop—that disconnects real people across the spectrum of real time by tethering them to their devices, where their peregrinations are recursive, self-directed, and inevitably closed. When Rebecca Mead published an article on what she termed "The Scourge of Relatability" in *The New Yorker* in 2014, it was only shocking because it was so long overdue.

The "me generation" did not, of course, erupt as a consequence of that *Harvard Business Review* article, even if we may think of it as a casualty, a fraction of the collateral damage of so much technology, so much of it personal, customizable, "me"-able—which is to say, selfishness-inducing. Nor could its authors have predicted the extraordinary impact that the concept of empathic design would continue to have, so long after its original publication—an impact that has revealed itself, to a large degree, as a catalyst for progressive thinking and engaged, conscientious change. Yet for every engaged design activist who has bravely pioneered this new terrain (and there are many), there remain scores of wannabe makers hacking their way through a culture of hypocrisy, practicing "empathy" while Instagramming their lunch, marching on Earth Day while BitTorrenting music, supporting their own interests at the potentially significant expense of others. This is a crisis not only of consequence but of conscience too; a failure of deeper understanding not about what it means to be a designer, but what it means to be a human being. And part of that means admitting that no matter how fast your connection speed, no matter how much you claim relevance and relatability as your defense, no matter how much you presume to think you know what is going on in someone else's life, you really don't understand a damned thing.

IN THE END, MY HUSBAND FOUGHT HIS CANCER LIKE A CHAMP. For seventeen months he hung on, a prisoner of pills and promises in that terrain of lofty optimism that is framed by the medical establishment— another industry that would do well to reconsider the importance of humility. Ultimately, there were no answers, only intermittent measures of fleeting hope—a clinical trial here, a respite of progression there—born of the protocols that turn us all into good little soldiers, each of us holding our breath and hoping for a reversal of fortune. In this solemn setting, the best little soldiers were our children, whose quiet perseverance during the vigil of their father's protracted illness was nothing short of astonishing. Later, when we had run out of options, the chief resident oncologist insisted on meeting with the children in person, to share with them the visual evidence of a pathology so grim that he could not put it into words. It was only then, peering at those tenacious, cloudy deposits on a scan, that we understood what the end actually looks like.

Ultimately, all illness is visual. We learn from an early age to cover our mouths when we cough, to look away from the infirm, for whom we reserve a respectful, if distant compassion. We view the sick as though their illnesses might be catching, and consider hospitals as remote but necessary sanctions, temporary holding cells for those whose afflictions are far greater than our own. Fearful of our own impending mortality, we bestow advice when we have none to give, a wishful display of our own imagined fortitude—which is actually the opposite of humility. (In those moments when you feel compelled to play misery poker? Don't.) We think we understand the pain or needs or hopes of others, but we do so with a kind of artificial distance, born of willful elitism, of fear and arrogance—as though any of it is controllable, let alone understandable, let alone truly fixable. (If sickness is catching, maybe wellness can be willed.) All of us are made from the same cells, all of us some combination of what Susan Sontag once called a "ruin of flesh and stone." To understand humility is to grasp that idea: mortality comes from being mortal, which means "belonging to this world," but it also means living—and it also means death. We would all of us do well to remember that design, no matter how cleverly conceived, or subversive, or disruptive, is never going to change that.

Chapter Ten: Memory

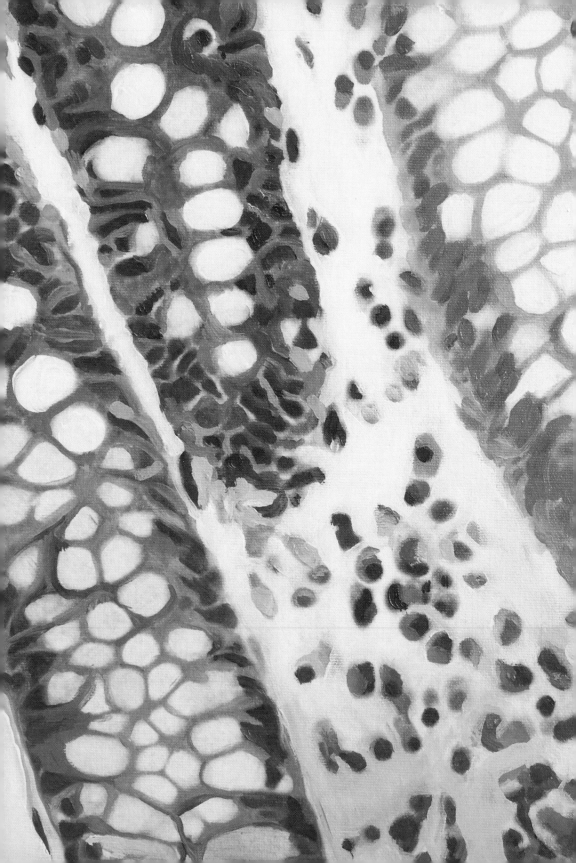

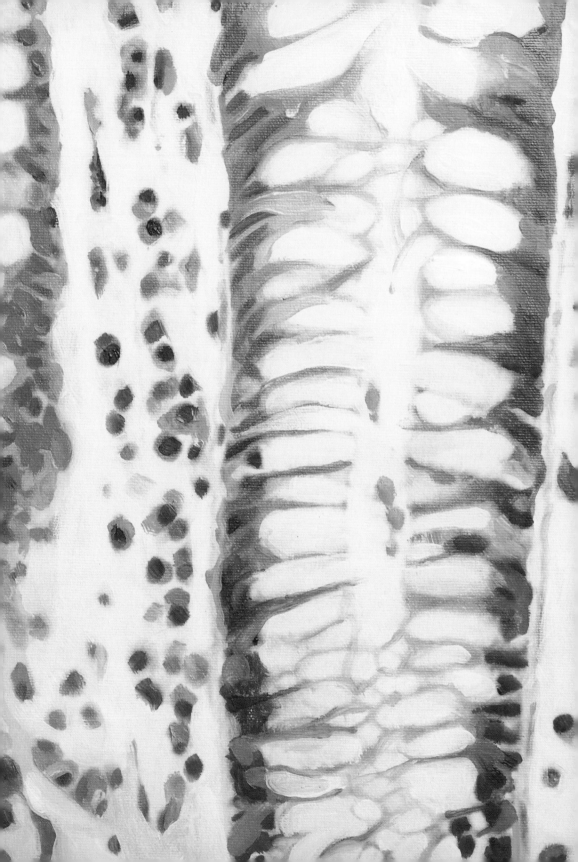

IN UMBERTO ECO'S BOOK, *THE MYSTERIOUS FLAME OF QUEEN LOANA*, the protagonist—a rare book dealer in Milan—has lost his long-term memory and soon retreats to his family's house in the country, where, surrounded by books, magazines, records, and photographs, he attempts to reconstruct his own lapsed self-history. Safe in home territory, he thus engages in a kind of archaeological dig of the mind, a personal journey in which visual stimuli become, over time, a series of precious land mines for memory retrieval. Curiously, and in spite of their glorious presence in the book, the inclusion of early twentieth-century specimens of paper ephemera reads as a separate narrative, a loosely gathered timeline of (in this case, Italian) graphic propaganda. These are memory prompts of the most precious kind: random yet piercingly redolent, disenfranchised from the present, dramatic and compellingly vivid.

Eco's versatility as a storyteller is most remarkably demonstrated in an early scene in which the protagonist's memory loss is challenged by a photograph of his own late parents. "You tell me these two were my parents, so now I know, but it's a memory that you've given me," he confesses to his wife. "I'll remember the photo from now on," he adds. "But not them." Images, particularly photographs, are immediate triggers for memory because they require no translation: we identify with them, see ourselves reflected in them, and digest them without effort. This may explain, at least in part, why so many of us are drawn to vernacular photographs, to street photography and documentary footage, images that in spite of their anonymity remain profoundly reflective of things we can recognize: places, moments, ourselves. Yet where would the artistry be if not here—making the everyday more memorable because of some formal slippage, some displacement that renders the usual anything but usual? The late art director Tibor Kalman once published a photo of Britain's Queen Elizabeth, impeccably retouched as an African American woman. Is this any different from the impact of Diane Arbus's Jewish giant, or Garry Winogrand's mixed-race couple with chimpanzees? You look and look again at something, and you remember.

One of the methods by which design affects the things we remember is through the act of defamiliarization—a term coined in 1917 by the Russian theorist Viktor Shklovsky that operates on the premise of presenting the everyday in an unfamiliar manner. This kind of intentional displacement is evident in the work of everything from advertisers (who want you to remember their products) to retailers (who want you to remember their brands) to anyone hoping to craft an enduring, penetrating message. But where photos are concerned, this is tricky: to the degree that a photograph itself is a reflection of the everyday, how do we make new meaning, find new form, tell new tales?

In the late 1960s the British experimental filmmaker Hollis Frampton made a short silent film from the "waste" footage he found at the beginnings and ends of rolls of processed film. Pieced together as a series of abstract paintings, *Palindrome* is a visual celebration of a cryptic vernacular; it's an important film in the avant-garde canon because, by liberating itself from classic storytelling, the formal language engenders its own narrative—a series of kinetic Rorschach tests inviting viewers to interpret things as they choose. This is form stripped to its core: in the context of such interpretation, we invoke our own conceptual apparatus to decide what is visual, pictorial, meaningful—indeed, memorable.

In a similar formal exploration, Bill Morrison's 2002 film *Decasia* revisits Frampton's experiment while challenging our expectations not only about form but also about what pictures can be; in so doing, it catapults us into entirely new visual territory. Like Frampton's, Morrison's feature-length film is a collage of found footage, imperiled by time and oxidized by age. Here the chemicals have eroded the surface of the celluloid, creating patterns at once real and imagined. With its choppy edits, its hauntingly mournful score, and its wondrous celebration of excavated film footage, *Decasia* is painterly, if monochromatic. Organic, but frenetic. But mostly it is new: a new way of filming, a new way of editing, a new way of visualizing a story about the past that recalibrates our expectations, our feelings, our memories.

The sheer tactility of the medium (something we consider often in painting but rarely in filmmaking and, given our increasingly digital habits, seldom in design) becomes itself a kind of provocative visual language, composed of bubbles and blips and scratches and striations, a tension between foreground and background, between negative and positive space (amplified not only by the score, but by the speed and sequencing of the footage as well), that creates a kind of meditation of pure form. In this way *Decasia* recalls the circle paintings of Eva Hesse or James Turrell's light sculptures. It's a body of work that engages the mind and enraptures the eye. And the stunning result is that we see something in an utterly new manner: part collage and part newsreel, old material presented in a new light. The effect is spectacularly haunting: it's a visual provocation.

Throughout this film there are tensions—some formal, others perceptual and even emotional—which both sustain the work and frame the viewer's experience of it: Slowness versus speed. New versus old. Ugliness versus beauty. Life versus death. As one becomes swept up in the fleeting narratives, so too do the visual permutations repeat and intersect, collide and recombine. Whirling dervishes and watery landscapes. Rope ladders and film sprockets. Births and baptisms. An eerily solarized courtyard at dusk. Did Morrison deliberately choose moments that lent themselves to such elegant abstraction? In this film, the graphic reality of the decomposing surface itself—and its haphazard intrusion upon the narrative(s)—raises the idea of graphic storytelling to an entirely new level and reframes, perhaps, the role memory plays in the context of visual media.

Arguably, it is precisely this that makes *Decasia* so compelling: the physical erosion of the film—in truth, it's a kind of visual autopoiesis, the film organically decomposing in front of your eyes and reemerging as something else—becomes a formal catalyst in the unfolding of its narrative. The film's decomposition becomes an intrinsic part of its identity, much as sand and dirt enshrine a recovered archaeological specimen. This kind of visual slippage is stunningly normal in everyday life but rarely exposed onscreen. Perhaps it is what Lawrence Wechsler calls "the wrenching persistence of the image... its refusal to die... in the face of the inevitable decomposition" that makes *Decasia* so unforgettable.

Unforgettable too is the idea that such decomposition is randomly generated: such lack of control lies at the core of contemporary media in general (and design in particular), in the sense that "experience" is ultimately controlled not by the designer but by the recipient. Artistry, in this view, is less about creative choices and more about curatorial judgment, more of an editorial than an artistic hypothesis. This film reminds us that memory is all about the forgotten moment, the chance encounter, the individual experience. Design engages them all.

IN THE LATE EIGHTEENTH AND NINETEENTH CENTURIES, MEMORY was understood as an indulgence, a weakness, even an affliction that was tantamount to nostalgia—which itself was seen as both a social phenomenon and an ailment to be cured. To many, nostalgia was a loose synonym for disease, with at least one doctor describing it as a "hypochondria of the heart." Over time it came to typify the porous romanticism of bygone eras—Victorianism, for example—a notion that conjured visual evocations at once sentimental and ornamental. The pragmatic reserve of the International Style would eventually succeed in diminishing the public's appetite for decorative excess, inaugurating an increased appreciation for streamlined simplicity and can-do progressiveness, a spirit we would later come to recognize as one of the key underlying hallmarks of modernism.

But the yearning for the past never really went away, perhaps because it remains such a human sentiment to miss something and to want to return to it now and again. Why else would we keep calendars and diaries and albums if not for some essential need to mark time? ("I can only note that the past is beautiful because one never realizes an emotion at the time," wrote Virginia Woolf. "It expands later, and thus we don't have complete emotions about the present, only about the past.") Such artifacts function as gestures of physicality and permanence: they're tangible, graphic reminders of our own evolution, evidence of our engagement in and with a larger, much more complex world. By the late twentieth century, nostalgia would begin to be summoned as fodder for satire: indeed, three years after making *Palindrome,* Hollis Frampton's 1971 film *Nostalgia* consists of a series of his photographs being ceremoniously burned on a hotplate, while descriptions of their contents are read aloud.

Memory, as it happens, is a fairly unreliable search engine. It's fuzzy and utopian, honoring an imagined past over a real one. As a consumer society we doggedly retain the handle "new and improved!" even as we hunger for its opposite: we want antiqued and weathered, a purposeful patina. Legacy looms large, heritage becomes a wishful aspiration, and memory becomes reengineered through an appeal to anything "old." In this view, "old" can be memory-inducing through its appeal to the analog and the authentic. (This is steampunk territory.) Words like "retro" and "vintage" appeal because they offer a kind of instant provenance—pedigree by proxy—a reference that is hardly restricted to the domain of the two-dimensional. Software programs like iMovie and Hipstamatic include "aged film" filters, lending your summertime theme park video clip, say, a palpable sense of Sputnik era panache. Architecture participates equally in this time-warp masquerade, with faux Tuscan, phony Colonial, and imitation Georgian arguably among some of the more popular styles in new construction. (Consider, too, the tony psychological profile promised by suburban residential enclaves identified by bizarrely fabricated and pretentious names—Fox Run, Heathcote's Landing—with developers packaging a pretend past, staging "heritage" one McMansion at a time.) In fashion, certain big branding conceits—Old Navy reviving the Summer of Love, for instance, or Ralph Lauren channeling F. Scott Fitzgerald—effectively mobilize nostalgia as a catalyst for sales, but it's patently clear that it's harmless, and besides, we're all mostly "in" on the irony. Replaying collective memory from a bygone era is a kind of theatrical improvisation: wear the clothes, play the part, have a ball. But some memories are more complicated: they're uncomfortable, inescapable—even grim. The ethics surrounding their visual representation are confusing, because the memories themselves are so fragile, so toxic. The bigger problem occurs when we don't want to remember at all.

IN 2008, FRANCE'S THEN PRESIDENT NICOLAS SARKOZY PROPOSED a new education plan in which every fifth grader would learn the life story of one of the eleven thousand French children deported and later killed by the Nazis. Fifth graders are, of course, only ten years old—a fact that prompted vociferous protest by legions of psychologists arguing that exposure to the horrors of the Holocaust would be far more traumatizing than instructive. The President's plan was met with vigorous disapproval from his political opponents, while both secular and observant Jews perceived it as morally reprehensible. "You cannot ask a child to identify with a dead child," argued

Simone Veil, a French politician, Holocaust survivor and the former president of the Foundation for the Memory of the Holocaust. "The weight of this memory is much too heavy to bear."

Meanwhile, scores of preteens routinely witness all sorts of horrors just by watching the nightly news. Films inevitably offer immersive, if fictionalized, accounts of all kinds of violence, corruption, and evil, while on television, the broad disclaimer "Viewer discretion advised" is as likely to precede a cable documentary on the dangers of high-risk pregnancy as a news feature on prison conditions in New Jersey. Equally paradoxical is the degree to which the film industry is predicated on the assumption—well borne out in box office sales—that we willingly pay to see scary movies that are scary only because their proximity to real life seems chillingly possible. Conversely— and paradoxically—Figure 1, a cooperative online photo-sharing app, offers anonymous, crowdsourced photos documenting a wide range of physical afflictions. The platform itself is public, and while only medical professionals can comment, anyone (yes, even children) can look. An image of a tooth abscess or a two-headed fetus may not, in and of itself, represent an emotional backstory, but the image itself may, to the unsuspecting civilian observer, be equally if not more difficult to bear than an image from a World War II prison camp. Whose discretion are we talking about here?

Meanwhile, the US Senate Intelligence Committee releases a report condemning the CIA's use of torture, while over in a parallel universe the proliferation of violent video games continues to reinforce the supposition that the use of force can be a good thing, and you can power up to the next level if you're tough enough. Hate crimes are tweeted, reminders of enduring racism are replayed through pictures in the media on all the sad anniversaries; yet in spite of the saturation of so many images that telegraph their no-nonsense messages (whether against abortion or anti-Semitism, apartheid or racism, makes little difference here), we become inured to them, visual memories playing repeatedly like just another car commercial.

Yet crimes against humanity are too hot to handle; ergo, we shouldn't teach the Holocaust to ten-year-olds by encouraging them to identify with other children, because that's just too close to home. To the degree that some of our most enduring memories are cued by visuals, what's the moral code at the core of these decisions, and who makes them? Human memory itself may be uneven, but pictures—whether born of casual observation or penetrating in their sheer madness—possess an inescapable permanence. This is a question not of happy endings, but of irrefutable ones.

In the spring of 2007, Seung-Hui Cho, a senior at Virginia Tech, shot and killed thirty-two people in what was the deadliest massacre by a single gunman in US history. Strangely, in advance of the rampage (and before taking his own life) the assailant managed to send terrifying images to the editors at NBC News, as though intending to both art direct the brutality of the event and preside posthumously over its unthinkable aftermath. The question of whether or not to publish these images was deeply controversial at the time, raising critical issues about newsworthiness and media decorum, and thereby reigniting the moral paradox at the core of all crisis reporting. In this context, publishing considerations—at once editorial and ethical—were (and are) critically tethered to what we see and remember.

Pictures of an angry twenty-three-year-old wielding twin handguns on camera are just as disturbing as the images of bodies hurtling out of flaming windows on 9/11. (Some might argue that because the killer himself both took and mailed the pictures to NBC, they were more disturbing.) It is perhaps fair to suggest that both events, along with the indelible imagery that will forever accompany them, have now been assured their respective places in the picture pantheon of modern-day tragedy. But does that mean they should have been blasted across the front page of every newspaper all over the world? And who decides?

Following the bombing of the Twin Towers on 9/11, the decision about whether or not to publish the photo of a falling man—graceful, upside down, unthinkably tragic—was handled in many cases completely differently outside the United States, where varied political, cultural, and religious positions framed a range of media perspectives. (Too close to home? Too far from home?) Efforts toward what the American theorist W. J. T. Mitchell would later refer to as "image amnesty" (literally, a call to forget) were—indeed, are—equally far-ranging, reminding us that pictures do not only speak louder than words but also are more likely to be remembered, simply because they are so impossible to forget.

While the decisions whether or not to publish such disturbing images may be determined by representatives of the media, these images are consumed by a public fully capable of an entire range of emotional responses, and one of them is that we are each entitled to remember what we *choose* to remember. True, there is no scientific method for anticipating the "right" reaction to something so horrific, but to deny its existence is equally, if not more, vexing. That the same essential questions plagued the media after the liberation of the Nazi death camps in 1944, or following the Islamic State beheadings in 2014, or any of a thousand times in between, does not make seeing these images any less confusing or any more comprehensible.

But when images are distributed through public media, at least we know what we're looking at. With the advent of citizen journalism, viral video, and blogging, this territory grows even murkier: truth telling, factual evidence, and reality itself are not so easy to identify, let alone assess. Where news media picture desks once ascertained credit and fact, today the free-form taking and sharing of casual pictures demands no such protocol. Thus the caption, if any, secedes from the image; the now decontextualized image floats about, unmoored from fact; and people remember what they choose or care to remember. (Or don't.) It is one thing if a picture is from your high school graduation, quite another if it has to do with 9/11 or the Ebola virus or the aftermath of a crazed gunman. Human memory is more than just fallible: it's intangible, difficult to pinpoint, virtually impossible to control.

Meanwhile, images—at turns cryptic and expository—engage our minds in ways both wonderful and weird. We take and make them, seek and share them, upload and publish them, distort and freeze-frame them. We see ourselves reflected in them and become, in a sense, callous to their impact, inured by their ubiquity. Indeed, we are all visual communicators now: even Seung-Hui Cho chose to tell his story through pictures. Mercifully, responsible news professionals remind us that veracity is a core journalistic value: words and pictures don't tell just any story, they tell *the* story—the real, raw, newly minted facts that need to be told. In this view, pictures of a gun-flinging madman may indeed have their place. But to the untold scores of people whose lives have been forever scarred by a senseless, incalculable human loss, such pictures are gratuitous and terrifying and mean, no matter how big or small or nicely cropped and aligned to a left-hand corner. Design cannot fix this. And it never will.

Chapter Eleven: Desire

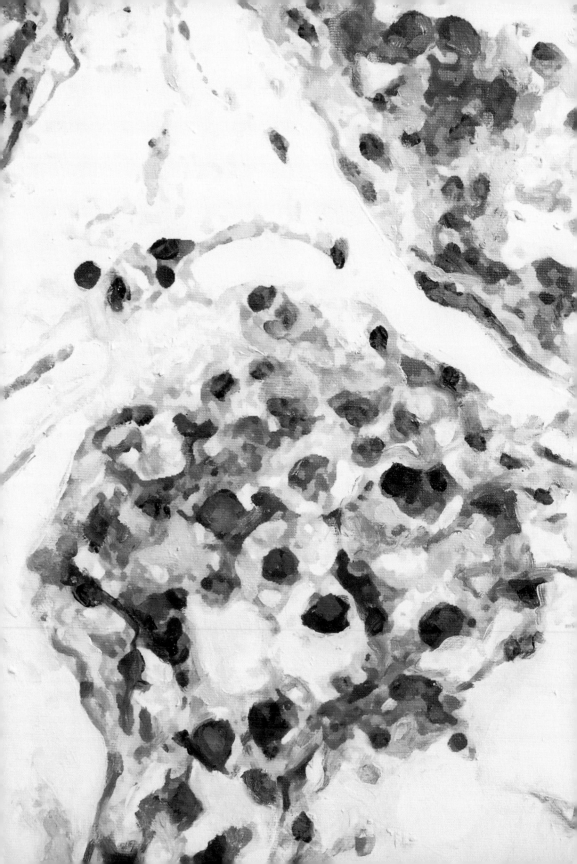

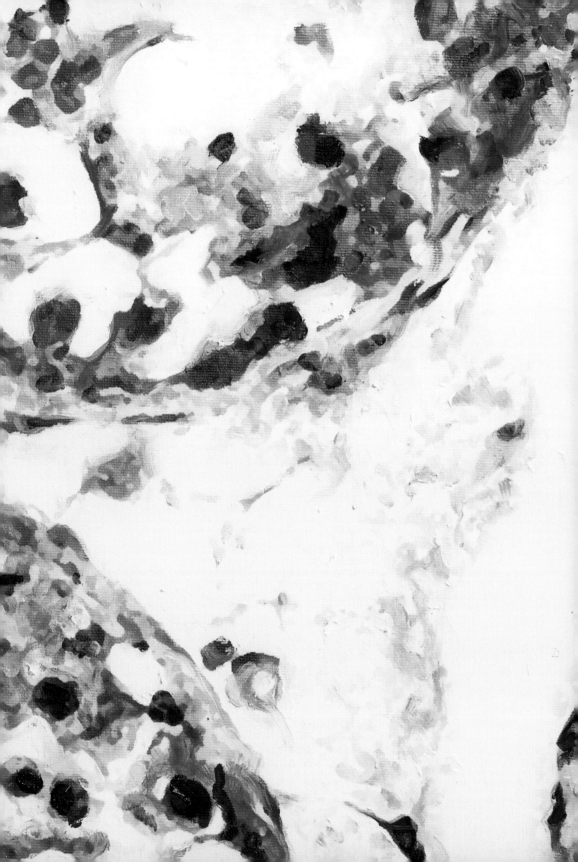

ONE AFTERNOON WHEN I WAS ABOUT EIGHT YEARS OLD, A BOY IN MY class gave me a box of candy—individually wrapped penny candy sticks, as they were known back them—in what I can only imagine was a gesture of kindness. Or flirtation. Or perhaps even love. I am reasonably certain that I had no romantic interest in the boy, but I melted inwardly at the thought of such massive quantities of candy within my reach. I also knew there was no conceivable way my parents would let me keep, let alone eat, any of it, given the sober realities of what was, at the time, our decidedly sugar-averse household. So I did what any other shamelessly calculating third grader would do: I sold the candy sticks individually to my friends, earning approximately nine dollars.

And then I bought a Barbie.

This brief anecdote speaks to many things—from the absurdity of illicit transactions on the black-market schoolyard, to the comparatively nonsensical dietary fascism of my family, to the way all of us inject profoundly personal meaning into inanimate objects—but mostly, it speaks to want. The things we want are part of an endless and endlessly shifting list informed by high culture and low culture, nature and nurture, whim and whimsy. Some things we want are practical: faster laptops, lower taxes, cheaper airfares. Some are wishful: flawless beauty, endless youth. Often the qualities framing our wants are mercurial, personal, and lean toward the hyperbolic: better, faster, cheaper. The role the designer plays in cultivating that want relies on numerous factors—some pragmatic, others seductive—making design practice a tricky orchestration of need (what the thing has to do) and novelty (convincing yourself and others that the best way to do it is with a new thing). To engage the eye while simultaneously lassoing consumer loyalty is the stuff of branding, but at its core it's all about an enduring desire that links a person to a designed thing, for as long as it is humanly possible to do so.

Why is desire such a compelling, all-consuming human need? And how is the practice of design complicit in the delivery of ideas and services, interactions and engagements, objects and promises, and so much more? For generations certain kinds of lofty aspiration were the stuff of science fiction, but more recently the fulcrum of want has successfully shifted from wishful to probable. Increasingly this is the purview of technology, and in particular of personal technology, and wearable technology, and embedded technology, and all sorts of technology we haven't even anticipated yet. That technology provides us with things, and that these things beckon with meaning, are the bedrock expectations upon which capitalism fundamentally rests, but they also inform the degree to which design can skew the emotional reach of need—whether desperate or playful, real or imagined, yours or mine. While desire can be a willful force, it can also be deeply irrational and, at times, frustratingly paradoxical. Therein lies its beguiling power to enchant—but also, it must be said, to deceive.

The word "desire" comes from the Latin, *desiderare,* meaning to long for, wish for, demand, or expect—a broad trajectory that aptly characterizes our relationship to and feelings about objects, from the loose pangs of longing to the bold drive of need. Desire can reveal itself as a passing craving or a full-tilt motivation, as lust or hunger—but how does the design process itself function within this mercurial narrative? In a capitalist society it is frequently impossible to divorce design from want, to disassociate the process of formalizing a thing from its intended objective, which rests upon its physical acquisition. (As a fundamental practice, design itself tends to be targeted, goal-oriented, and pragmatic: it's about making stuff.) Yet the question of taste makes defining desire a near-impossible task. Identifying the qualities that convey that adrenaline-rich emotional punch—the factors, simply put, that motivate desire—is what designers often aspire to do, obliging us to conduct an almost epistemological leap into the material unknown.

The study of evocative objects is at once a curatorial process, a social behavior, and a function of scientific inquiry. The American chemist and peace activist Linus Pauling believed that science was a search for truth, a way to try to understand the world. Might the same be said for design? ("This involves the rejection of bias, of dogma, of revelation," Pauling wrote, "but not the rejection of morality.") A generation ago we understood things within the broader scholarly rubric known as "material culture," but the core psychological drivers that connect us to wanting things have, in recent years, moved well beyond the grounding of tangible items. (Google's "material design," a so-called "visual language that synthesizes classic principles of good design with the innovation and possibility of technology and science," is its unlikely twin: here materiality is identified as a system, the raw material for things rather than things themselves.) Today things inhabit platforms and services, feeds and tags, all of them traceable via coordinates and metrics that swirl around us in a haze of updates and backups and drones, where finding, making, appropriating, sharing, and even eliminating something altogether can make the concept of want a highly transferable commodity. A political candidate trashes her e-mail and is barraged by public doubt and scrutiny. Cryptic strings of code are auctioned at a museum, like art. Today things can seem invisible but remain eternal. We may not always be able to see or touch them, but they perform for us. Surveillance, it seems, never sleeps.

This is of course particularly evident in digital spaces, where what we've come to identify as the Internet of Things addresses the connectivity of things to code, embedded strings of data that can now support networks of more and more things so that they are capable of exchange, retrieval, and archiving in unprecedented ways. These anticipatory responses of code-embedded objects promise improved services, enhanced speed, and increased watchfulness—which in the case of, say, a monitoring pacemaker is a good thing. (In the case of covert surveillance, maybe not so much.) On the other hand, in an age of purposeful transparency, where open-platform sharing is quickly becoming the norm, the ethical dimension of this sort of anticipatory engagement raises serious concerns about privacy. Because that's a thing, too.

As totems of memory and meaning, things beckon because they're cues to who we are. Many writers—including, but not limited to, Sherry Turkle, David Rose, and Donald Norman—have examined our complex relationships to and with things. Norman in particular has written at length about the behavioral responses that characterize our relationships with inanimate objects, noting that because these connections derive from learned experience, we attach expectations to them—often highly unrealistic expectations—which explains why only yesterday you cried out in despair when you dropped your laptop, or misplaced your car keys, or, in my case, managed to drop your iPhone into the toilet. (Don't ask.) Perhaps the problem isn't the misalignment of exalted expectations so much as a skewed concentration on cause and effect. If the failure of objects to live up to our expectations is a modern-day consequence of our reliance on the digital, why do we focus on the transaction over the expectation, the thing more than the impulse? And if the subject matters less than the sentiment, why isn't the process as—if not more—compelling than its highly anticipated promise? If, indeed, expectation is a learned behavior, why not change *that*? While the modern world continues to produce objects that may, at any moment and for whatever reason, ensnare our desire—from the territory of the battery-operated toothbrush to the market for musically responsive vibrators to the future of self-driving cars—this is not now, nor has it ever been, a question of what but rather a question of why.

DESIRE IS ONE THIRD OF THE PLATONIC TRIFECTA: TOGETHER WITH emotion and knowledge, it's what defines all human behavior. It's an intrinsically human need, an emotional and spiritual and idiosyncratic set of complex drives that only partly rest on patterns of consumption—but more than anything else, it is the existence of these patterns that tethers desire to design. We can crave connectivity, or sugar, or sex; we can want a chocolate chip cookie or a brand-new computer or an afternoon indoors with a good novel; or maybe, following a particularly grueling winter, we just want some sun. We want to be happy and fulfilled, challenged and entertained, safe and satisfied, but perhaps most of all, we want to be in control: of ourselves, of our destinies and our future. So we leapfrog from task to task, reinforcing a sense of self-perpetuated "comfort" by outsourcing to services and systems and devices that pretend to do just that: switches and buttons and apps and tools, remote controls on timers that turn on the lights or water the garden or pay the bills. Priding ourselves on a kind of amped-up, decentralized efficiency, we inject value into the thing that helps us get there, our fidelity directed to the prop rather than to the person.

To the degree that visual appeal is a significant catalyst in what we believe we need, design functions across a set of highly volatile variables, made even more elusive because so much can be customized at will: tags and filters function as dispassionate colanders, grouping like-minded "assets" and trying to take the guesswork out of choice. The compelling, if mildly disturbing, concept of "anticipatory" design proposes the idea of deploying creative thinking to diminish the ambivalence that comes with option paralysis—choice perceived as a burden rather than a benefit—which carries the notion of groupthink to an entirely new and worrisome level. This may not represent surveillance per se, but the idea that your patterns are traceable—whether they're shopping patterns or spending patterns or even romantic patterns does not really matter—makes privacy a highly endangered commodity. Things themselves are triggers, and the feelings they imbue in us—from longing to lust—are difficult to pinpoint, because in spite of what marketing experts want us to believe, they're profoundly unstable. It is one thing to love your children, quite another to cleave unwaveringly to a chair, or a typeface, or even a smartphone. The fulfillment of desire rests on many things, not the least of which is timing.

Certainly this explains the vicissitudes of pleasure, which have partly to do with exhibiting patience but have mostly to do with managing expectation: watching and waiting and paying close attention. Design frequently locates itself in the material, and design choices themselves operate on multiple levels, reflecting what are, not infrequently, paradoxical ambitions: we might crave measures of economy along with gestures of excess, or seek a sense of mystery alongside a feeling of security. None of these inclinations are in fact measurable; yet all of them stem from the capacity for choice, which lies at the heart of desire, and is, for that matter, our most fundamental of sentient prerogatives. (It's what separates us from other primates.) Anticipation, in this context, is part of life.

To want something is to convince yourself you need it. Or you deserve it. (Or both.) To this end, the line between connoisseurship and consumerism is tenuous: taste, ever personal, trumps the arguably trickier role of good judgment, and the ethics of choice are instantly exposed. My children were outraged recently when I chose to buy a preowned Mini Cooper instead of a brand-new electric car. No amount of argument on behalf of budget (mine) or range anxiety (mine too) or even the resultant relatively low impact on the planet (mine again—after all, this was a Mini, not a Cadillac Escalade) swayed their opinion of me or of this decision, which was in their view a pitch-perfect example of social irresponsibility writ large. Their mother was the enemy who privileged design over duty. Simply put: if you want something badly enough, you can convince yourself you need it. And while a great advertising campaign may result in higher sales figures, or a beautifully designed concert poster may lure more ticket buyers, the cause-and-effect relationship between desire and design does not always manifest through such simple, quantifiable transactions.

There are many tales of what might be called desire run amok, all of them rife with visual cues that raise alarming questions about the democracy of choice in the pursuit of desire. Adults, we are told, are increasingly turning to professional photo retouchers for their family photos, lest a random blemish tarnish the illusion of perfection as their children's likenesses are reproduced on holiday cards or broadcast across social media. A retired editor hosts docent-led lectures at her new gallery, where her well-heeled clientele are advised to take the $5,000 they might spend on just another handbag and invest in an artist instead. And a misguided, if well-intentioned, parent who throws a party for a child based on the theme of Roald Dahl's famous book *Charlie and The Chocolate Factory*—by hiring a number of adult dwarves to literally impersonate Dahl's Oompa Loompas—is stunned when the prepubescent guests are so terrified they hide in the supply room for the duration of the festivities. No matter that in the original story itself, the greedy children are voted off the island first, or that the ensuing result privileges the poor but honest protagonist. Here the visual trumps the actual. Design may matter, but in the absence of good judgment, we're doomed.

Each of these examples represents a twisted path: from inappropriate notions about delight to misaligned expectations about outcomes to warped values about money. The fulfillment of physical acquisition stands at the core of all of them—"want" in its purest, most unadulterated state—and with each the point of entry is, in essence, a visual one. Doctored photographs. Overpriced handbags. Oompa Loompas. Visual literacy is not the same thing as media saturation, need not the same as greed. Desire, whether fueled by personal pleasure or by public propaganda, manifests in aesthetic choices that are inseparable from the ethical dimensions framing our lives, defining what it means to be a responsible, self-actualized, morally grounded human being. In other words, just because you can doesn't mean you should.

Owning things inevitably involves money, and money is personal. Yet so are gender and class, education and nationality, notions of leisure, feelings of worth, the lure of greed, our yearning for mystery, and our eternal, epic struggles with guilt. And in between lie a host of other factors—cultural, political, and ultimately, deeply personal—the essence of which both drive and determine the success or failure of the thing itself. Curiously, design—so often a synonym for making things—can sometimes be responsible for eliminating them too. We cannot talk about want without understanding loss. So what happens when our things go missing?

FROM JULY 19, 1977, TO FEBRUARY 28, 1981, THE SECURITY STAFF AT New York's Roosevelt Raceway on Long Island kept a fastidious record of lost property. The result—152 pages of wayward mittens, misplaced wallets, and hundreds of personal items—is as much a record of the social history of a generation as an inventory of wayward stuff. There are the wallets—once called billfolds—believed to have resided in overcoat pockets or ladies' purses, and often described with their contents: credit cards from now defunct metropolitan department stores like Alexander's and Ohrbach's. There are the eyeglasses—once called spectacles—characterized by their size, tint, and designer signature—Vidal Sassoon, for example. There are countless garments, most, though by no means all, of them jackets and coats. (There is at least one report of a lost shopping bag containing two pair of boys' boxer shorts and another, logged merely as "the loss of underwears.") And then all at once, in between the umbrellas and the car keys and the ankle bracelets, there is the poignant report of a set of missing false teeth in a green purse, a detail that one can only imagine was intended to help differentiate them from all the other reports of missing teeth found that day. (Shockingly, there were none.)

Teeth, however, don't even begin to describe the oddities reported at Roosevelt's track, flea market, and casino—where, on March 20, 1978, someone reported a lost box of Girl Scout cookies and a book entitled *Physics for Career Education*. Several weeks later, a local resident claimed to have lost $2,350 sometime between buying a pretzel and the top of the tenth race. Elsewhere there are missing baby clothes (who takes a baby to the track?) and wedding rings, a birth certificate, a blue-and-orange-flowered plastic bag, mimeographed copies of important files, and a woman's faux fur coat: "Right pocket contains a lot of keys and left has lipstick."

This leads us to the descriptions furnished by the patrons, at least one of whom possessed a rather extraordinary capacity for visual recall. A certain Miss E. Leung of Tudor City lost a brown leather bag with corduroy grooves and a metal clasp: fair enough. But when asked to describe the contents of her bag, Miss Leung reported the following: "Driver's license, check books, credit cards (about 11) and keys (2), address books, cosmetic bag, wallet with about $35 cash, tax exempt card, ball pen, package of cashews, package of pistachios, two bus tickets to Lakewood, New Jersey, date book and private mail." According to the log, the bag was never recovered, leading one to wonder: might its owner have fared better by taking a more minimalistic approach—just reporting a missing wallet, say, and some nuts?

In all likelihood, Miss Leung probably responded as many of us would, guided by the assumption that greater detail is an asset—at once a reflection of one's capacity for memory retention and a more persuasive strategy for an item's recovery. Indeed, from the perspective of those recording the lost items, one cannot help but linger over the descriptions themselves—detailed yet oddly dispassionate, almost scientific in their tone. Others are weirdly cryptic and, as befits the style of the perfunctory log, punctuation-free: "Black mans rain hat size 7 ½ left in security office by unknown." (Was the man black or was the hat black?) Occasionally a concerned officer attempted a drawing of a piece of jewelry, a poignant characteristic of a book otherwise notable for its inventive spellings. (On the typographic front, at least one of the security scribes added circles over her—or his—lowercase i's.) Found items were stapled to government-issue green domestic return receipts—Postal Form 3811—with copies returned to the relieved patron. Though most were lost belongings, the occasional stolen item typically enlisted the involvement of a higher-up, a sergeant or, in one instance, "The Chief."

Then there is an entry recorded at about 4 p.m. on October 26, 1980. While the officer on duty did not attempt a sketch, the verbal description offers an unmistakable glimpse of the physical characteristics of one particular patron's loss: "Carol Thaler of Great Neck lost beige pocket book shaped as a pig," notes the officer. "Please mail if found."

The Raceway staff were, by all indications, a meticulous crew, a group of men and women who took their custodial jobs seriously and served with pride—without judgment, without gratitude, without computers. Back then, in the macramé age, a generation or two before the luxuries of spell checking, a small group performed a tedious yet highly necessary task. Yet today, nearly half a century later, their diligence provides us with a written record of an entire lost demographic: it's a tribal report, the work of accidental anthropologists. True, we can mock the accidental loss of a teddy bear or an umbrella or even a diamond-encrusted faux-crocodile watchband, but who are we to judge those who felt it necessary to travel to a racetrack in possession of these trinkets, such seemingly random beacons of meaning and value and love? Today we can trace missing packages as easily as we can mail them, but apart from the digital facility with which we navigate our orbits, the relative value of the missing thing (or the missing person) remains as personal—and as idiosyncratic—as it ever was.

The story of lost property is the story of material culture seen through a different lens, a world characterized not so much by things as by the *absence* of things: a world in which what we acquire has as much resonance as what we abandon, where one man's hat is another man's heirloom. The Roosevelt Raceway's lost-and-found ledger reads like a screenplay—character driven, conflict-rich, and full of truly bizarre period detail—but more striking still is the fact that it's an intensely visual record with virtually no visual data. Outlandish in places, endearingly captivating in others, it's a distinct part of social history—and maybe a key part of design history—that's been long lost. In an age in which things continue to occupy a central role in our understanding of contemporary culture, documents like these also deserve to be found.

IF BEAUTY IS INDEED IN THE EYE OF THE BEHOLDER, THEN WHY DO WE rely on market research to tell us not only what people want but also what that want looks like? Consider, for example, the paradox known as "look and feel." On a phenomenological level, we could ask ourselves whether what I see as blue is what you also see as blue, and then arrive at a semantic clarity (agreeing to disagree?), but this is old territory. The professionally observant neurologist and writer Oliver Sacks claimed he had seen the color indigo only twice in his life, once in a museum and the other time only because he chose to *summon* its presence, an act that could only be achieved under the influence of staggering quantities of recreational drugs, which raises the question: can desire be willed? Barring excessive drug use, and assuming that in the absence of pharmacological experimentation such perceptual ambiguity is probably harmless, what about this thing called "feel"—and how do we begin to explain it? Is it even remotely possible that something so amorphous and so deeply personal can be calculated, quantified, and packaged, or are we just agreeing to agree? So quantified is the essence of "look and feel" that corporate mandates can now protect them from easy replication. (We have the litigation teams at Apple, Microsoft, and Hewlett-Packard to thank for that.) Still, these metrics have, for a number of years, come to characterize the desirability of design: while look is something tangible, it's the feel part that's so elusive—and even though there is an entire global industry of human factors engineers and user interface specialists to tell us with empirical precision what drives intuition, the whole idea of "look and feel" remains something it may never be possible to pin down.

Because we are groomed to transmit more than we receive, and because designers are by nature committed futurists, it's not now, nor has it ever been, popular to think this way. The late American graphic designer Paul Rand was famously resistant to anything that smacked of group-driven creativity, believing that the consensus building required of such practices—focus groups, market research—was anathema to the creative process. (And as much as he believed that "everything is design," Rand would have deplored the notion that everyone is a designer.) But he was a man of pragmatism too, and he likely agreed with his friend and client Steve Jobs, whose own views on "look and feel" were equally critical. ("It's not just what it looks like and feels like," Jobs famously quipped. "Design is how it works.") Nevertheless, this concept of "look and feel" remains a mainstay in the digital sphere, where beautiful things are desirable because they are efficient and portable, shiny and sleek. User testing is no longer an optional activity but rather an integrated part of modern life, of digital culture, indeed, of design itself. When you find you can no longer separate form from function, that's where the problems start.

Occasionally, it seems, there's an ineffable sense of impending doom to making design: you think it, you create it, you disperse it, and then... where does it go? Typically, it has a slow evolution, an embryonic migration from idea to thing, or from a single thing to many things. Or it splits, mutating into subparticles of things, colonizing at a cultural level, like slang. Or it boomerangs back in some way, informing the design of yet another thing.

(We call this progress.) Sometimes design extends its abbreviated journey from thing transmitted to thing received, but in general the designed thing is intended to have a rather targeted life. If it did not, there would be no succession to new and improved things, and no economic imperative for growth. While this may not constitute planned obsolescence per se, it does indicate a life cycle that's not entirely mindful of our capitalist tendency toward waste. Why else would we have coined the phrase "upgrade eligibility"?

It might be argued that design that endured over the course of the past century often did so because of its appeal to a kind of basic homogeneity: simply put, it achieved timelessness by removing itself from the specific. Consider the Swiss-born Adrian Frutiger's design of the humanist type family Univers; the Italian-born Massimo Vignelli's identity program for the National Park Service in the United States; or the Uruguayan-born Edward Johnston's type design for the London Underground—updated not long ago by the British designers Banks and Miles but, to the average person, fundamentally unchanged from its original inception in the 1930s. Together these examples testify to the great modernist paradox: the International Style was, in fact, not international in the least. What it was, was neutral.

But desire is not a neutral emotion. We may yearn for structure or systems, reliable benchmarks upon which to graft our physical expectations, convincing ourselves that subscribing to such codified evidence anchors us to some sort of empirical truth, some reality that extends our worthiness, our capacity, even the clarity of purpose that we believe characterizes our lives. So we pride ourselves as "early adopters" of technologies or services that "brand" us as progressive and smart. Or we only buy food labeled "organic" (whether it really is or not is perhaps debatable) because it makes us feel good about our engagement with the earth. Or we photograph and share our meals in restaurants, believing that capturing enough ephemeral moments cements us, by sheer force of habit or methodical effort, to some carpe diem we have yet to truly locate.

In the modern world, design has become democratic and universal, which at once boosts and eviscerates its value. It has become a thing in and of itself, a machine for making: a vehicle for delivering messages, taping performances, mapping services, extending communications, and affirming storage capacities. If we yearn for devices, it is because we have convinced ourselves that ownership of such devices virtually liberates us from the burdens of a task-driven existence. If our desire to buy and own things that free us from toil is what fundamentally marks this generation from the last— or, for that matter, the next—then we persist in these choices at our peril. Desire is emotional and messy, idiosyncratic and anything but rational. The things that we want make us who we are, and if we all want the same things—or worse, if our desire for those things shepherds us down the same path to uniform desire—then the fulfillment of the International Style may reveal itself as a truly dystopian legacy, hardly what we hoped. Desire may lead, but must we follow?

Chapter Twelve: Change

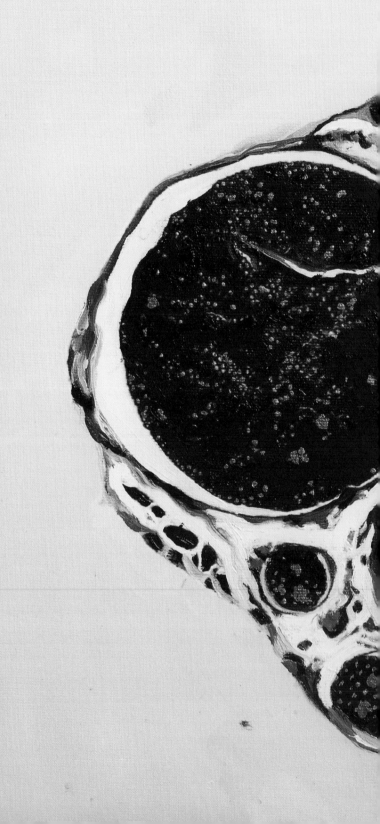

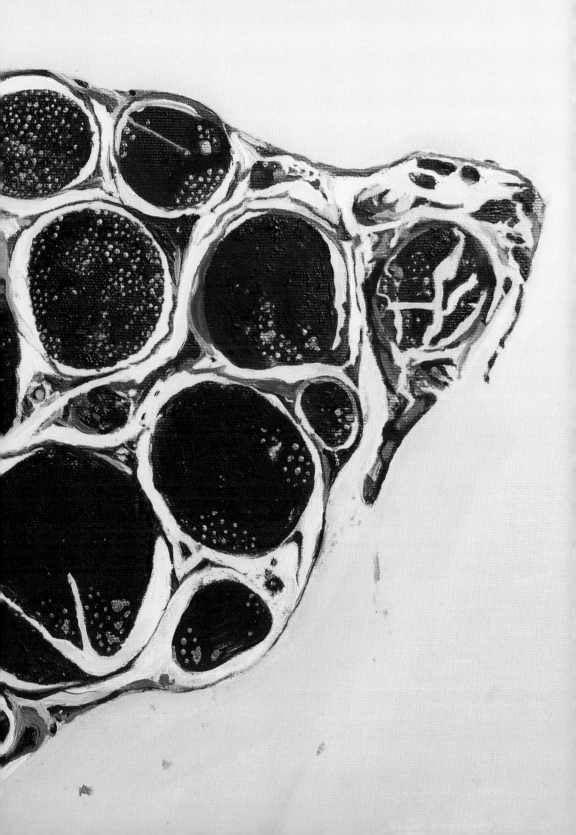

STRAIGHT UP THE WEST AFRICAN COAST NOT FAR FROM CAPE TOWN, South Africa—past Namibia and Nigeria, beyond Angola and Cameroon—sits the Republic of Ghana. It is a small country, about the size of the state of Oregon, with a constitutional democracy and a population of just under 30 million. Over the course of the last thirty years, poverty in Ghana has declined, but a fundamental lack of infrastructure—access to economic opportunity, to agricultural production and food security, among other things—has slowed progress on multiple fronts. Only a small percentage of Ghana's roads, for instance, are paved, making transport (indeed, making everything) more onerous for its inhabitants, many of whom are refugees from other African countries.

I recently met a taxi driver who emigrated from Ghana fourteen years ago and has not returned since. A college graduate, he is the eldest of seven and has single-handedly financed all their educations: on his watch, each of his siblings has gone to university. One brother is a physician. Another is in graduate school. A sister studies in the United Kingdom. The impact this man has had on the lives of his sisters and brothers is a result of tremendous sacrifice, but even more than this, it is because of his remarkable character. His example illuminates the degree to which change remains so piercingly human, even or perhaps especially in an era marked by its exaggerated preoccupation with our increasingly external definitions of what constitutes success and productivity.

The degree to which designers self-identify as agents of change is founded upon a premise that's noble, if fundamentally flawed: how is it that the material evidence of our efforts has come to define our ambitions rather than our humanity, our personhood? My chance encounter with one remarkable man on a snowy afternoon in New York was a reminder that at its core, change happens when you reset the coordinates for someone else. Maybe that's not a design story. But it should be.

APPROXIMATELY THREE THOUSAND MILES SOUTH OF GHANA, THE NINE provinces that constitute the Republic of South Africa cup the bottom tip of the continent, occupying a landmass that's roughly an eighth the size of the United States. Following colonial independence from Britain and decades of apartheid, it remains a complex society, particularly in terms of its relationship to its sub-Saharan neighbors, many of whom are struggling with serious economic, political, and health challenges. The World Health Organization reports that South Africa still holds the top position globally for HIV infections and deaths, at 17.3 percent. Nearby, in Central Africa, some 5.5 million people have died in the Democratic Republic of the Congo in the last twenty years, mostly due to poor public health conditions. (Half of those victims were under the age of five.) The 2014 Ebola outbreak was the largest viral epidemic in history, affecting multiple countries across West Africa. From Somalia to Sierra Leone, worldwide life expectancy statistics place the inhabitants of African nations at the bottom of the heap. And while reported deaths by malaria have been steadily decreasing in recent years, ninety percent of the global total in 2013 was on the African continent.

In an age in which visual literacy is understood to be a core competency for most of us, it is staggering how little we know about the world beyond our own immediate borders. These statistics about Africa do not tell the whole story, even as they represent a set of metrics, random nuggets of data that provide a way in to those of us scanning the bullet points that purport to be news. Those metrics, like the neutral, codified visual language of maps and charts that accompany them, are mere graphic approximations of a story. But what story do they tell? Think of Western elections and their 24/7 news coverage, of pundits and predictions that frame our understanding of parliaments and politics, and ask yourself: Will improving charts help? Will infographics enlighten voters? Can design really change any of this? In spite of a wealth of access to the tools of communication that enable us to access pictures and news feeds and video clips, we're all of us armchair tourists, perched on the outside, peering in.

Recent reports that the steep decline of the Kenyan economy may be closely tied to the collapse of the coastal tourism industry raise critical questions about how we perceive a place from the outside. In Kenya increased joblessness, idleness, and poverty have resulted in grim prospects for its nearly 45 million inhabitants. Travel advisories—which have been issued repeatedly over the past three years, in the wake of a series of highly publicized terrorist attacks in Kenya—have served, among other things, to alienate prospective travelers, significantly weakening the once-vibrant coastal economy there. Travel advisories are nothing more than warnings, and warnings are critical to communication: as such, they are the currency in which designers must trade. Just as we turn to news sources to alert us to safety recalls, viral epidemics, and other public dangers, inclement weather conditions depend upon travel advisories to minimize danger where visibility is key. And perhaps it is precisely this—the very idea of *visibility*—that makes the act of warning a design problem. To warn is to protect from harm, a function of image and language, scale and hierarchy, timing, strategy, even scare tactics. To what degree do design choices impact safety precautions, wayfinding systems, the critical ramifications of prescription intake? Can warnings about terror become acts of terror themselves, gestures of communication in which the perpetuation of fear itself becomes, in fact, a lethal weapon?

The realities of the Kenyan economy reveal themselves in lost jobs and despondent workers, empty beaches and stalled tourism: unemployment spurs nefarious activity, and the terrorism cycle reignites once more. "Terrorism," Christopher Hitchens once wrote, "is the tactic of demanding the impossible." To demand what *is* possible, on the other hand, implies a reasonable and humane set of conditions that might well be pursued in the name of design. To look, and listen. To watch, and wait. To understand that service to others is not a reflection of your own values but stems instead from capacious empathy, profound understanding, and the kind of patience that is largely ignored in contemporary life. This is what it means to grasp the idea of design as a humanist discipline: inviolable and principled, compassionate and responsive.

IN THE LATE SPRING OF 2015, THE HIGHLY RESPECTED NONPROFIT Architecture for Humanity (AFH) filed for bankruptcy. Their own informal tagline—"Design like you give a damn"—was inversely proportionate to their extraordinary mission: that everyone deserves access to the benefits of good design. Advocates for design as empowerment, crusaders for human rights, they proved over the course of fifteen years that design really matters. (Or at least it did matter.) Still, we can't perceive this as failure, as their efforts were hard-won and thoughtfully executed, demonstrating, among other things, that the designer's role as a catalyst for change begins with a fundamental humility. This approach stands firmly at the opposite end of the kind of long-standing imperialistic colonizing that for so long characterized "help" from the West, decades during which those more fortunate would torpedo in with an arrogant, and inevitably flawed, understanding of what kind of change was needed, let alone what was realistic, even actionable. AFH advocated for local and collaborative solutions, sensitively conceived and empathically executed—observing, for example, that "vulnerable communities rarely benefit from top-down solutions brought in by outsiders." True, design may have played a formative role in these initiatives, but the decisive role was a human one.

Within a day of Architecture for Humanity's filing, an op-ed commentary appeared in the *New York Times* that was coauthored by George Clooney. Did the world pay more attention to the crisis in Darfur because this story was tethered to a celebrity? Perhaps. But before you judge this as a savvy media play, consider this. Clooney and his coauthors looked at Sudan in general (and Darfur in particular), and their links to their own nonprofit, the Satellite Sentinel Project, have proved a seriousness of purpose that is at once sobering and smart. No: they're not designers. But their platform is stunningly visual: it's about looking, watching, seeing—and taking action, in this case, by deploying pictures to document human rights violations in Darfur and elsewhere. Their own brilliant tagline— "The world is watching because you are watching"—makes all of us agents of change, reminding us that to be human is to be vigilant, a word that comes from the Latin, *vigilantia,* "to keep awake."

That designers want to make change is a noble ambition, if not a realistically actionable one. While there is strength in numbers—which explains why connecting ourselves to existing NGOs and established nonprofits may be the most appropriate behavior and indeed, our most realistic option—we ultimately act alone, each of us reflecting upon the moral and ethical choices by which we lead our own lives, independently, one at a time. We make change when we admit, first and foremost, what we can't change, which means accepting our limitations, whether cultural or economic, religious or geographic. "Everyone thinks of changing the world," wrote Tolstoy, "but no one thinks of changing himself."

This is what it means to strip away pretense, to understand design as a function of who we are, not what we do. Detached from hyperbole, removed from the machine-dominated enterprise of modern culture, design is to civilization as the self is to society. In the end we are all of us sentinels, crusaders pursuing the promises of achievement in the name of progress. As the architects of our collective future, that progress will be hopelessly stalled without a deeper embrace of personal vigilance, ennobled by character, generosity, and grace—all qualities we must champion in ourselves and in each other. To truly advance as a civilization of design-minded individuals is to embrace the hard-won capacities of the human soul, remembering that we are people first, purveyors second. Design may provide the map, but the moral compass that guides our personal choices resides permanently within us all—and it is here that we begin to see design for what it really is. To embrace design is to spark novelty, improve livability, expand opportunity, streamline productivity, leverage capability, massage readability, but perhaps most importantly, it is to engage humanity. And we do this best by being human, ourselves.

Index of Paintings

EYE CAPSULE

A strong, transparent membrane protecting the lens. The membrane itself is thin, but elastic: such tension creates a spherical shape for the eye which helps to support structure and focus.

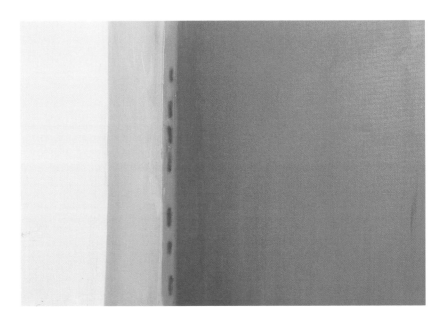

TEASED NERVE

Nerves are coated with a myelin sheath to increase the speed of electrical impulse propagation. The teased-fiber technique is used to see, and thereby better characterize, suspected changes in tissue sections.

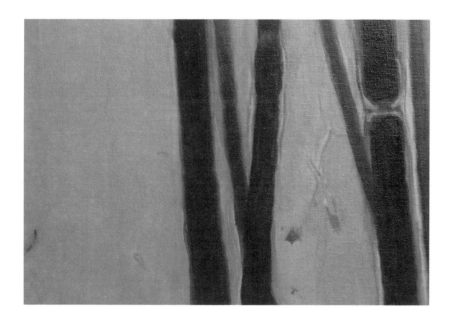

EYE CHAMBERS

Scientists at Oxford University recently identified the portion of the brain where the conscience—literally, the region governing our choices—actually resides. Unique to the human brain, the lateral frontal poles (there are two of them) are located just above each eyebrow.

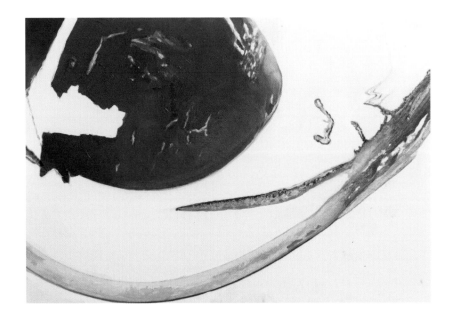

PITUITARY GLAND

Considered the "master" gland, the pituitary is a hormone-producing gland located at the base of the skull that regulates multiple functions within the body. It does this by secreting hormones into the bloodstream that govern, among other things,metabolism, blood pressure, and growth.

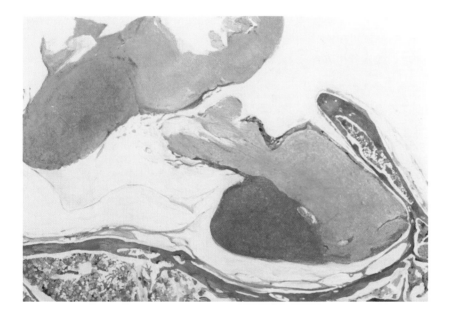

PINEAL GLAND

Often referred to as the third eye—Descartes called it "the principal seat of the soul"—the pineal gland, located behind the brain's third ventricle, is part of the epithalamus, which connects the limbic system to other parts of the brain. It produces melatonin, which both anticipates and regulates the circadian rhythms of certain physiological functions (including sleep and sex). Excessive doses of melatonin have been known to increase the likelihood of vivid dreams.

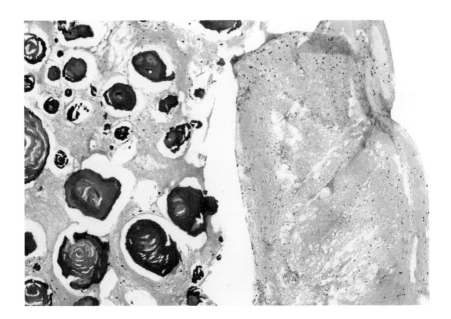

BONE MARROW

Producing some 200 billion new blood cells every day and occupying on average four percent of the total body mass, bone marrow is housed within the medullary cavities within the bone. It contains red and white blood cells and their progenitors along with stem cells that can become all the supportive tissues of the body including blood vessels, fat, cartilage, and bone.

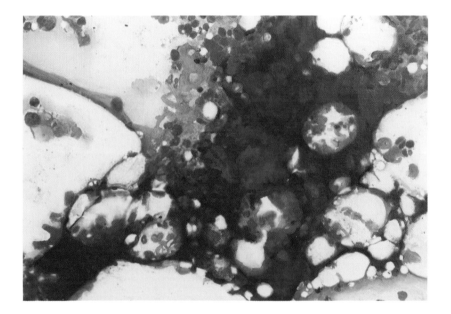

CONSEQUENCE   **LYMPHOMA**
The lymph system is part of the immune system, which helps
the body fight infection and disease; lymphoma is a group
of blood cancers that develop in the lymphatic system. An
unregulated cellular proliferation involving the immune
system's white blood cells can lead to lymphatic cancer.

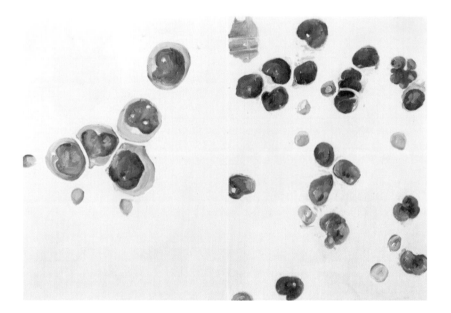

05

COMPASSION

HEART VENTRICLE

Connected by valves, the human heart has four chambers, of which the lower two are called ventricles. In a normal heart, the right ventricle has an easier job, since it pumps blood only to the lungs: its muscle is usually not as thick and generates much less pressure than the left ventricle.

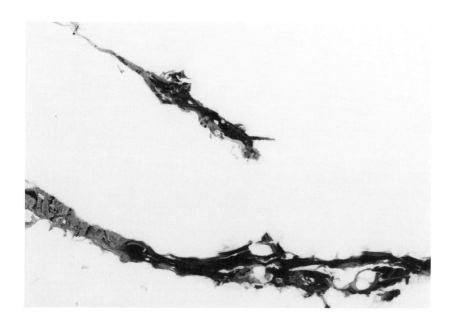

PATIENCE

HYPOTHALAMUS
An almond sized brain structure serving as the neural link
between the brain itself and the hormone-producing endocrine
system, the hypothalamus is critical for homeostasis—the
maintenance of the body's internal environment, stabilizing
equilibrium between interdependent elements of the human
body. It influences nervous control of all internal organs, and
regulates endocrine function, electrolyte and fluid balance,
even involuntary behavior.

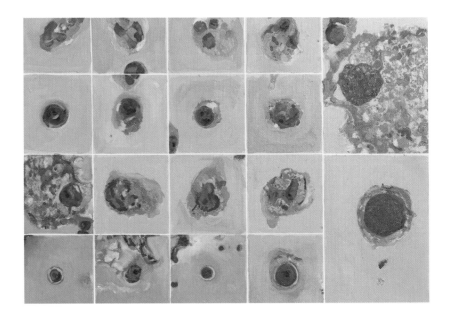

MITOCHONDRIA

The so-called powerhouse of the cell, the mitochondria are the working organelles that generate chemical energy. These microscopic power plants generate chemical energy in the form of a molecule called ATP that fuels cellular reactions. Composed of two membranes and host to their own particular DNA, mitochondria store calcium for cell signaling activities, generate heat, and mediate cell growth, differentiation, and death.

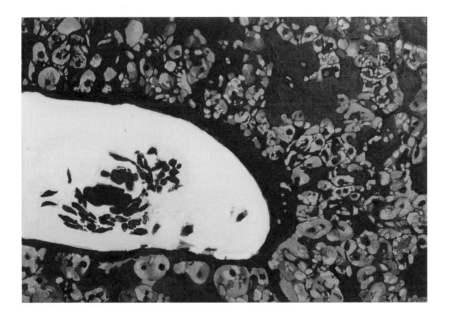

MACROPHAGE
A macrophage is a large, specialized cell that recognizes, engulfs, and destroys target cells. Known for their plasticity, these cells can change their functional phenotype depending on the environmental cues they receive. They play a central role in the immune response to foreign invaders of the body (such as infection) and because they can literally sense danger, they are also involved in the removal of cellular debris.

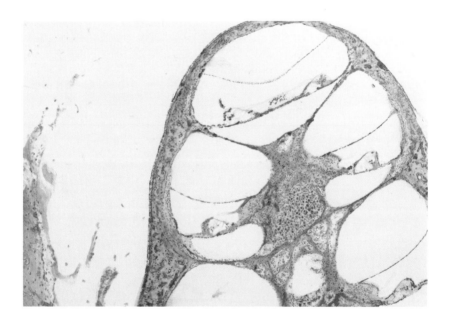

MENINGITIS

Meningitis is an inflammation of the meninges, or the three membranes that envelop the brain and spinal cord. This can be caused by infection, tumor, trauma, or autoimmunity. Mollaret's meningitis, pictured here, is a benign (non-cancerous) meningitis believed to be associated with the herpes simplex virus.

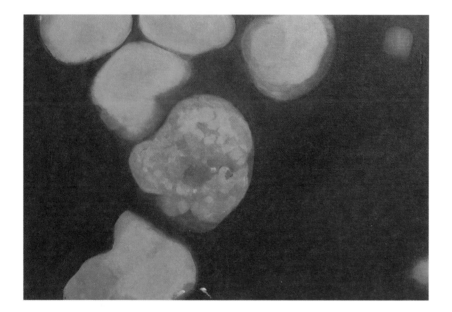

MEMORY

INTESTINE

The gut is host to a complex community of microorganisms—the microbiome—where intestinal bacteria have a direct correlation to brain activity including mind, mood, and memory.

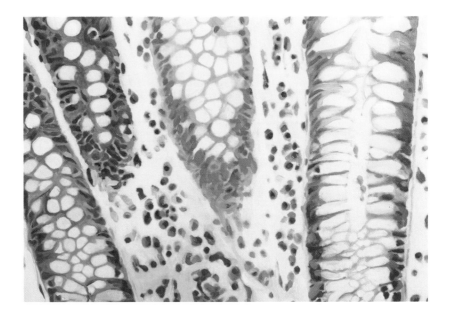

DESIRE

TESTES

From the Latin, testiculus—meaning "witness" of virility—the testes are the essential organs of the male reproductive system, the endocrine glands where testosterone is produced.

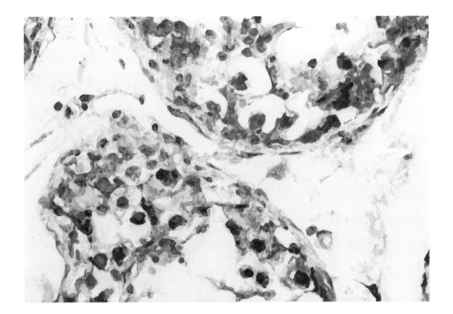

MYELIN

Myelin is a core membrane layer of lipids, fats and proteins that coats, protects, and insulates the nerves. It's purpose in neural communication is to enable the swift and efficient transmission of electrical signals. Loss of myelin is a problem for many disorders of the central nervous system including stroke, spinal cord injury, and multiple sclerosis.

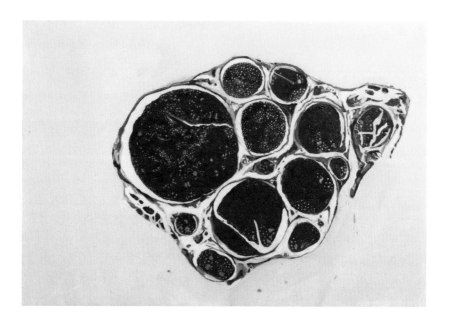

I AM GRATEFUL TO MANY PEOPLE FOR THEIR SUPPORT WHILE THIS BOOK was being written, beginning with my superb team at Yale University Press: Steve Wasserman, who conceived of the idea for a book that might examine the now ubiquitous role that design plays in everyday life, and who gracefully guided this manuscript; Jeff Schier and Duke Johns, who patiently edited it; Eva Skewes, who made the process feel more seamless than it actually was; and Chris Coffin, who can be depended upon, always, to make me look better than I am.

Portions of this book appeared in earlier incarnations on Design Observer, and I am especially grateful to my colleagues there for their support: special thanks to Eugenia Bell, Michael Bierut, Betsy Vardell, and especially Sara Jamshidi, my deputy in picture research and scientific translation, as well as all things design-related. Sheena Calvert, Liz Danzico, and Blake Eskin were early readers, and the book benefited deeply from their collective insights and constructive suggestions.

The visual body of work for this book would not have been possible without contributions from a number of people who deserve particular mention, beginning with George Baier IV who generously photographed my paintings. Joanna Radin encouraged my hunger for biological imagery. Matt Grant provided medical oversight. Rick Prum was my scientific sounding board, and Ann Prum my greatest cheerleader. Jen Renninger lent her support from the trenches of her own studio, my curator from afar. My longtime friend Catherine Waters saw this body of work before anyone else, and encouraged me to connect it to the ideas in this book. And Paula Scher cheered me on throughout, my greatest supporter and champion.

In the pantheon of friends, Kevin Hicks and Cornelia Holden loom especially large: for their spirited conversation, humor, and enduring support I am most grateful. My thanks also to John Dolan, Dr. Paul Fiedler, James Gleick, Melissa Harris, Steven Heller, Siri Hustvedt, Maira Kalman, Noreen Khawaja, Hamish Muir, Laurie Simmons, Stefan Sagmeister, Alan Thomas, and Timothy Young. In Paris, where much of this book was written, my thanks to Anette Lenz, Véronique Vienne, and Lucrezia Russo. In addition to my peers at Yale, I am grateful to Rebecca Ross and Rebecca Wright at Central Saint Martins in London; to Catelijne van Middelkoop and Ryan Pescatore Frisk at the Design Academy Eindhoven in the Netherlands, and to Andrew Howard at the Escola Superior de Artes e Design in Porto, Portugal. Working with students at these institutions has been an immense gift.

Finally, to my dearest children, Malcolm and Fiona Drenttel, and to my father, William Helfand, my gratitude in all things, always.

Jessica Helfand

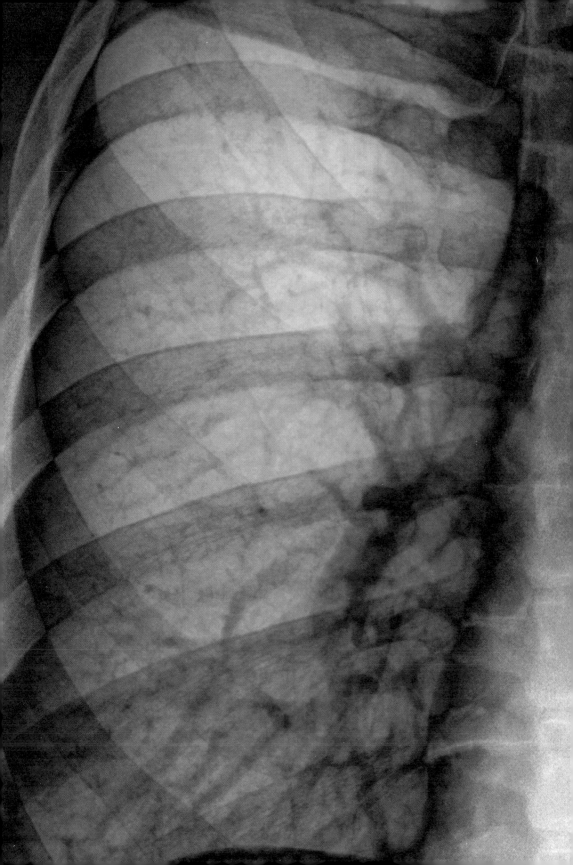